WARTIME ENCOUNTER WITH GEOGRAPHY

Also by H. J. de Blij

Africa South (1962)

Mombasa: an African City (1968)

The Earth in Profile (1977)

African Survey (With A. C. G. Best) (1977)

African Perspectives (Ed.) (1981)

Wine: a Geographic Appreciation (1983)

Wine Regions of the Southern Hemisphere (1985)

Earth 88: Changing Geographic Perspectives (Ed.) (1988)

Nature on the Rampage (Ed.) (1994)

Harm de Blij's Geography Book (1995)

WARTIME ENCOUNTER
WITH GEOGRAPHY

Harm de Blij

The Book Guild Ltd
Sussex, England

The Book Guild Ltd,
25 High Street,
Lewes, Sussex

First published 2000
© Harm de Blij 2000

Set in Times
Typesetting by IML Typographers, Chester, Cheshire
Printed in Great Britain by
Bookcraft (Bath) Ltd, Avon

A catalogue record for this book is
available from the British Library

ISBN 1 85776 457 9

CONTENTS

ACKNOWLEDGMENTS

This book owes its genesis to the staff of ABC Television's *Good Morning America*. In June 1994 the programme, then by far the leading early-morning programme in the United States, broadcast from the beaches of Normandy to commemorate D-Day, the Allied invasion of 6 June 1944. I had served since 1989 as *GMA*'s Geography Editor, and with maps and charts I tracked the advance of Allied forces from the beachheads on the French coast.

During my discussion with Joan Lunden I remarked that I had been in a small village in the Netherlands when the invasion took place, and described the hope and strength it gave us during the Nazi occupation. My producer, Jane Bollinger, suggested to Executive Producer Bob Reichblum that *GMA*'s upcoming remembrance of the end of the Second World War include a segment about my wartime experiences, including the day of our liberation on 5 May 1945. Bob agreed, and told me to start making preparations.

During and immediately after the war my home address was Julianalaan 1 in a village then known as Soestdijk, and in the autumn of 1994 I wrote a letter to that address, introducing myself, explaining that I had lived on those premises during and after the war and asking whether the present owners would allow me and the *GMA* crew to invade the house on 5 May 1995. I received a gracious letter from Mrs J.C. Nederlof-Feij inviting me and *GMA* to spend the day at the house. 'By the way,' she wrote, 'this address still is Julianalaan 1, but no longer Soestdijk. We are now part of the municipality known simply as Soest. You'll find many other changes.' On behalf of the family Z. Nederhof she offered any help we might need.

My day in Soestdijk (using the old name) was an emotional experience. In the early morning, while celebrations were going on in many places, the superb producer of my segment, Barbara Koster, suggested that we visit the Soester Museum, but it was closed. Following a phone call the curators, Mr and Mrs G.M. Backelandt, were kind enough to come to the museum and give our camera crews time to film some of the special war exhibits built especially for this day. They gave me access to files and photographs (some of which are reproduced in these pages), and talked with me about their own wartime experiences.

At Julianalaan 1, Mr and Mrs Nederlof put up with all the commotion a television segment entails: cables, lights, window blackouts, microphones, blocked hallways, open doors. 'Spontaneous' spots actually are done over and over again, until the producer is satisfied not only with content but also with pace, lighting and camera work, and we disrupted the house most of the day. Then, as it was time to leave so that the editors could put the segment together for broadcast to America (and the Netherlands) on 8 May, the Nederlofs sprang a huge surprise: they had found some of my schoolmates of 50 years ago and invited them to meet me. It was a day never to be forgotten and I am grateful to all beyond measure.

I also thank Charles D. Gibson, then the co-host of *Good Morning America*, for doing the 8 May interview with me during which the edited tape was run. Always in television, much more material is prepared than can be shown, and the pressure on airtime was enormous. But Charlie's interest in it ensured its presentation, and the avalanche of mail it engendered proved how effective Barbara Koster's work had been.

Many of the letters I received suggested that I write up the story in greater detail. For more than half a century I have kept a box full of letters, diary entries, newspaper cuttings, photographs, and other items relating to my wartime experiences, and my parents, in their nineties as I worked on this project, helped me fill in some of the gaps in my memory. This book tells the story of my wartime childhood, but it also chronicles my first exposures to the wonderful world of geography. By the time the war ended, I was enamoured of maps and geographic writings, and was eager to learn more about this subject in school. Next, I had the good fortune of having a truly superlative teacher in geography, and before my years in the Netherlands ended I had decided to become a geographer.

I have not regretted that decision for an instant; my professional life as a geographer has taken me to all corners of the world. My research projects have taken me from the rift valleys of Africa to the vineyards of China. I served as editor at the National Geographic Society and, after *Good Morning America*, as Geography Analyst for NBC News. I have held university positions from Washington to Hawaii. My books, judging from the mail, now stimulate a new generation to pursue geography. For having made all this possible, I thank all those who are mentioned in these pages, and especially my parents.

H.J. de Blij

1

TIME AND PLACE

The office that registers births, deaths and marriages in the city of Schiedam, a suburb of Rotterdam in the Netherlands, reports that I was born at 0700 hours in the early morning of 9 October 1935. The timing probably explains why I have never been a morning person: I was obviously unable to get over the experience of having to start life at dawn. I have friends who get up *before* dawn and who get to their offices shortly after sunrise, and they tell me that they actually enjoy those early hours. But most of them, it turns out, were born at a sensible time of the day, at mid-afternoon or early evening. Their biological clocks were set more favourably. Just think (as I often have): a life without a morning struggle to make that train, bus, class or appointment.

More than 50 years later I had the ultimate comeuppance for a late riser. ABC Television appointed me to the staff of its breakfast programme, *Good Morning America*. Whenever I got on the air, this meant a 5 a.m. wake-up call (sometimes earlier). No matter what I tried, it was a struggle. Coffee. Aspirin. Large breakfast. No breakfast. One of my students, in this age of equality and candour, said that I looked like I had just been shot out of a cannon. He was right. I never looked at any tape of my appearances again. It was jet lag without the jet. Fortunately the producers at *GMA* considered the message rather than the messenger, and my series survived nearly seven years, until the image-conscious Disney people, who bought ABC in 1995, put an end to my early mornings.

My birthplace was not a hospital room, but my mother's bedroom, as was the custom of the time and place. The family record shows that a physician came to help; a bowl of hot water was the sole medical back-up. Hospitals were for the sick; barring complications, babies were born at home.

My father took the doctor's certificate of delivery to the town hall that morning, to register me by name. For many generations, the first name of the first son in the family had started with an H, and there was no middle name. My grandfather's name was Herman. My father's is Hendrik. Mine was to be Harmjan. But when he wrote it that way on the appropriate form, a clerk, in the unmatched tradition of Dutch busybody bureaucracy, insisted that two names could not be combined. It was to be Harm Jan. My dad, in an uncharacteristic moment of mellow compliance undoubtedly related to the healthy arrival of his son, did not argue, and came home with a birth certificate that read Harm Jan de Blij. 'Doesn't matter,' my mother reportedly said. 'We'll call him Harmjan anyway.'

That would have been fine in Holland, where Harm has no particular meaning and Jan is the equivalent of John. But later in life, in the English-speaking world, I rued that moment many a time. Marshall McLuhan wrote that 'a man's name is a numbing blow from which he never recovers'. I never saw it that darkly, although there were times when I thought seriously of changing mine. In the late 1960s, a movie entitled *In Harm's Way* appeared and was advertised on theatres and billboards. For years afterwards, and to this day, there were people who could not resist the obvious quip. I had a dean at the university where I was then teaching who never failed, in personal conversation or public meeting, to ask whether we were doing things in Harm's way, or putting ourselves in Harm's way. I wished him just that, but kept my peace – and was saved in the most unlikely way. Before long a book appeared under the title *I Never Promised You a Rose Garden*. Almost immediately the dean, who once remarked that he was too busy to read books, began ending virtually every conversation, whether it dealt with budgets, curricula, tenure or football, with the phrase 'I never promised you a rose garden'. I was no longer in Harm's way. How good it is that our society sustains universities where such intellect may be nourished and rise to the top at taxpayers' and parents' expense.

Years later, when my career moved from academics to television, my first name, flashed on the screen as I appeared, became an issue again. Among the 7 million viewers who watched *GMA* in those days, thousands were moved to write to me over the years, the overwhelming majority with informative, sometimes amusing letters. A few who disagreed with what I might have said about Iraq or the West Bank or South Africa would write to Dr Harmful, or Harmless, or Harming, or other such appellations. My executive producer, Jack Reilly, suggested that I use initials only. It was good advice. I have done so ever since, from television to scholarly book covers.

Two factors made me keep my name, awkward as it may seem. First, a family member skilled in such matters managed to trace the family lineage back to the fourteenth century, and found that the family name had changed by only one (now lost) letter, an 'e' at the end of it. Second, our name has a wonderful meaning. In Dutch, *Blij* means happy, glad, joyous. When I go back to the Netherlands, my passport or business card almost invariably evokes a smile, joke or question. 'Are you always happy, sir?' What could be better?

In fact, I *am* in good spirits most of the time; even my wife Bonnie says that I am rarely in a bad mood. I attribute this to her, for she radiates happiness wherever she goes and has brought immeasurable joy to our lives in every home we have made during our long marriage. But personal and professional happiness do not always coincide, and in this respect I have been doubly fortunate. I have a love affair not only with her but also with the profession I chose even before I finished high school: that of geographer. My first exposure to things geographic occurred during the Second World War, in my parents' library of books, globes and atlases. Through the darkest and hungriest days of that period, geography gave me hope: I read of distant, peaceful cultures in warm climates where people were happy and free, where food was plentiful and travel unrestricted. I planned imaginary journeys to Africa and Asia, even started a diary to record what I would have seen. Almost literally, geography threw me a lifeline, showed me a way to get through the cold and the fear I describe in the pages that follow.

3

My second brush with geography came when things in post-war Holland began to return to normal, and I went back to school. At the Baarns Lyceum my daily curriculum included a geography class taught by a spellbinding teacher, a man who had travelled the world and who had survived the war in what was then still the Dutch East Indies. He had been in a Japanese concentration camp, but he made very little mention of that; instead, he told us of the wondrous cultures of Bali and Flores, Madura and Borneo. He had seen China and Australia and South Africa, and he drew maps on the blackboard that you would never find in an atlas. He fired my imagination and made me wonder why other subjects were not even half as interesting. By the end of my first year at the Lyceum, aged 12, I knew what I would want to be: a geographer who could write like Hendrik Willem van Loon and teach like Eric de Wilde.

On Wednesday, 9 October 1935, the Netherlands must have seemed far removed from the world's trouble spots. I have often talked with my father about his impressions of the time. The Nazis were consolidating their grip on Germany and threatening their neighbours, but Holland had remained neutral during the First World War, and many Dutch seemed to think that the Germans would not menace their country this time, either. In any case it was the Italians, not the Germans, who were making the headlines in the autumn of 1935. Italian armies were closing in on the Ethiopian town of Aksum. On 8 October, Mussolini roused a huge crowd in Rome with threats of a mighty Italian sword that would strike those who dared interfere with Italy's colonial campaign. The League of Nations was meeting to organize international sanctions against Italy, but not all European leaders agreed. George Lansbury, leader of Britain's Labour Party, resigned over his party's support of such sanctions, bringing to power Clement Attlee, who would defeat Winston Churchill in the aftermath of World War II.

If not in late 1935, then certainly in 1936 and 1937 it would have become obvious that Europe and the world were heading for war. Why did my parents stay in the Netherlands when surely they saw it coming? They owned no significant property, had no

4

business to anchor them to Rotterdam, and could make their living virtually anywhere in the Western world – or so it seems in retrospect. My father sees it differently. Crossing the Channel to England would have meant leaving family, losing friends, abandoning students, abrogating two rising careers. Economic times were tough. 'Your mother and I had worked too hard to end up as refugees in a foreign country,' he would say. 'Besides, the Germans seemed to be looking east, not west. I'm sure I would have left Czechoslovakia, or Poland, if we'd been living there. But Holland?'

And so I grew up in the shadow of the swastika, unaware that an idyllic childhood could end at any moment. For nearly five years, my parents' decision seemed to have been the right one, but by the time the warning signs grew stronger, it was too late. We were trapped, and eventually life for my parents became not a struggle to succeed, but a battle to survive.

2

GOOD TIMES

Recent research in psychology and related disciplines has begun to confirm what I have believed all my life: that humans (and probably other primates too) begin to learn and remember things while still in the womb. I certainly had every opportunity to do so. My parents are professional musicians, and their house was always filled with the sounds of practising, rehearsing, and sometimes chamber-music concertizing. My mother, a concert pianist, had a beautiful voice and seemed always to be singing when she was not playing. When I was five, she took me to a performance of the opera *Carmen*. During the second intermission, she says, I turned to her and asked why I already knew the songs I was hearing. 'Because you were born with them,' she answered. She may have been closer to the truth than she knew.

My mother was a pianist and piano teacher whose work ethic never faltered; she practised with a self-discipline unmatched, I think, by any of her students during her lifetime. In her nineties now, she still spends as much as four hours each day at the keyboard, playing a repertoire from Bach to Bartok with an energy and accuracy that would be the envy of an artist half her age. My father was a successful violinist who at the age of 17 was (and remains) the youngest player ever to hold a chair in the Rotterdam Philharmonic Orchestra. He later became concert master of two orchestras and retired as conductor. He, also in his tenth decade, likewise continues to practise four or five hours per day. In 1995, when he was 88, he played a programme of Sarasate and

Wieniawski aboard the cruise ship *Royal Viking Sun*, by special invitation, and proved that he had lost little of his technique. He got a standing ovation.

In the late 1930s our house in the Lange Nieuwstraat was filled not only with music but also with artists. Students came for their lessons, colleagues came to play chamber music. My room resonated with the discordant sounds of strings, winds and piano. In the evenings my father and mother often rehearsed sonatas together, and the melodies of Mozart and Schubert were my lullabies. A string quartet gathered twice a week to practise in the room right next door to mine, sessions that had been going on since before I was born. I loved those evenings from the moment I became conscious of them, but I had strong preferences when it came to repertory. Always I have had deep, visceral reactions to certain pieces of music, whether listening to them or playing them myself, and I think I know why. I got to know them before I was born. One day when I was four, I asked my father's quartet if they would play 'that Mozart piece with all the joy in it'. They played something that wasn't it, and I ran off crying.

Some other recent research suggests that playing and listening to classical music, notably Mozart, helps the brain and especially improves mathematical abilities. I am living proof of the exception to that rule. I have grown up and lived with Mozart's music, and maybe it helped with my arithmetic. But not my mathematics.

My other vivid memory is of the sunshine that poured into our windows, from one side in the morning and from the other in the late afternoon. The house was large, spacious, bright and airy, a three-storey town house with high ceilings and large, sunny windows. In the front, it overlooked a street lined with mature oak trees, beyond which lay a park with manicured lawns, gravel walkways and a large, circular pond, in the centre of which stood an elaborate fountain. All this was meticulously maintained by the city, whose crews were out daily, trimming lawns and sweeping paths. On Sundays, people by the hundreds put on their best clothes and promenaded in the park, the ladies in long dresses, sometimes carrying umbrellas or pushing baby carriages, the men in suits. I have seen French Impressionist paintings that could have been done here. It was a graceful, civilized scene.

My parents avoided the park on busy days like that. Crowded places, I learned early on, were not for them. But I loved sitting at the window and watching all the movement and the colours. And when the park was quiet, the street was busy. There was never a dull moment on, or across from, our street.

From the rear windows of our house you could see part of the port of Schiedam, whose waterway led to the great Maas River and out to sea. There was a quay to which boats and barges lay tied up, and goods in crates and boxes and barrels were loaded and unloaded. It was a never-ending, always-changing spectacle, complete with noises made by machinery and men and smells coming from cargoes of spices and coffee and cocoa. When a boat sailed towards the river, the drawbridge down the road had to be opened, and the traffic jam in front of our house would last for half an hour. I soon learned when to leave the back of the house and take up my position by the front window.

Many of my memories of the late 1930s are of walks with my parents through this beehive of activity, and of my excitement at being in the midst of it. A few doors up the block, towards the drawbridge, was a warehouse so large that it had doors on our street and a dock on the waterway. Cargo arrived by horse-drawn wagon and truck from the street, and by boat from the waterway. A team of horses could pull a fully loaded wagon all the way through the middle of the building to the water's edge. If you were there at the right time, you could see an incoming wagon pass an outgoing one inside the warehouse, so large was it. The rushing and shouting of the workers, the straining of the horses and the cracking of whips, the screeching of iron-rimmed wagon wheels against the cobblestones, the noise of the cars, the stampede of bicycles, the smells of roasting coffee and cacao – there was continuous sensory stimulation here.

The warehouse also gave me my first reality check, the first disappointment I can remember. When I was four, my mother allowed me to go by myself to watch the scene, and the men at the warehouse got to know me by name. That was a big, almost daily adventure, especially when the company dog produced a litter of five puppies. She lay in a bed of straw and was looked after by each shift of workers. As they grew bigger, the puppies began to walk around, and my mother sent me over with bits of soft food whenever I went, which was every day the weather allowed it. Soon the puppies had names, and the mother let me touch them. And then one day I arrived, food in hand, and the puppies were gone. So was the straw bed, and the mother. I ran over to some of the men who knew me so well, and asked where they had gone. All of them walked away. I tugged at the sleeve of one of them until he stopped. 'Don't know, kid,' he said, and lit a cigarette. I walked back past the place where they had lived, and thought how ugly and lifeless the concrete floor was where the straw bed had been, and what a difference those dogs had made in that rough-and-tumble warehouse. I never set foot in the place again.

But one tough lesson, one disappointment in more than four years, is not a bad record. Most of my days were filled with many kinds of excitement. There were, of course, never enough walks in the park, to the waterfront, to the shops, never enough tram rides (the town had just been linked to Rotterdam by tram), never enough visitors and music. My seat by the front window made up for this. And our window, like that of all others along the street, was fitted with a fairly large mirror (rather like today's exterior rear-view car mirrors, only larger), so you could see down the street without opening the window. Many a time I would spot my father, violin case in hand, far away in the crowd, coming home from a rehearsal.

My parents gave many public performances, but I was never taken to them. In fact my earliest memory of my father performing was on the radio – and it was not a violin concert, but an oboe recital. He had taught himself to play the oboe as a music-school requirement, and familiar music by Handel and Cimarosa emanated from the tiny radio on the music-room table. To prove that I was not yet in total touch with reality, I reportedly clapped hands when the concert finished, and said 'All right, dad, you can come out now.'

Of all these wonderful days I have spotty memories, although I am certain that my preference for city life and my love of music originated in this period. If there is a more stimulating way of becoming aware of the world, I do not know of it. My parents allowed me to bang on the piano, try a small violin, blow into a borrowed flute. My father let me 'help' in his tool-laden workshop. There were stacks of picture books, and many games, most of them of the building or construction variety. My grandfather, who was employed by the Netherlands Railways throughout his life, gave me a train set that expanded with every birthday and Santa Claus Day (Christmas in those days was still a religious holiday, and gifts were given on Santa Claus Day, 5 December). On the other hand, I saw very few children of my own age. Ours was an adult household, and from very early on, I could tell what was expected of me. Discipline was strict. But there were plenty of ways to keep myself occupied. If all else failed, I had a favourite rocking horse, to whose rhythm I sang the harmonies I had heard during practices and rehearsals.

That rocking horse almost cost me my life. I used to ride it while my mother was cooking dinner, in a spot in the kitchen where I was not in the way. If she was in the mood, she would sing an accompaniment to my melody; we got pretty good at the slow movement of the Bach D Minor Concerto for Two Violins. One evening in the autumn of 1939 I had spent more than an hour riding and singing, and at about 7 p.m. we sat down in the dining room. About ten minutes later there was a deafening crash that shook the house. My parents ran in opposite directions to see what had happened; my father thought that a car had come through the wall on the first floor, my mother assumed that one of our pianos had crashed through a ceiling in the back. The kitchen was the last place anyone checked. But there it was: a huge hanging cupboard, loaded with glasses, vases, dishes and other things, had come loose from the kitchen wall and had crashed onto my rocking horse, cutting it in half and splintering it. Almost the entire kitchen floor was littered with broken glass. I understood why my mother wept at the sight. Just think of all those broken dishes.

By the winter of 1940, outings with my father were regular and exciting events. Sometimes he even let me ride with him on his motorbike, sitting on his lap astride the fuel tank. He was enormously proud of his 1930 Royal Enfield, not as big but much better, he said, than a Harley Davidson. Riding it he would wear a thick leather coat that made him look twice his size, and I could lean back into the folds of it as we rode.

In his youth, my father had developed a great interest in biology and had collected specimens in boxes and jars, keeping a careful record. His parents, however, were not enthused by the growing assemblage of beetles and leaves, and made him dispose of it. Taking up the violin, he told me later, was his way of getting even. In his working-class family, if a biologist was unacceptable, a musician was unthinkable. But he persisted against all odds, made his way through music school, and launched a successful career. Yet he never lost his interest in natural history. And he made sure that I would have the opportunity he did not.

Just one tram transfer from our house was Rotterdam's city zoo, old and cramped but colourful. I cannot recount the number of times we went there, but it was an adventure every time. The noise in the huge bird house, the smell in the reptile house, the threatening looks of lions and apes, the patterns and colours of giraffes, zebras, cheetahs, tigers.

But I was not the most disciplined of zoo-goers. At the entrance gate you could buy peanuts for the monkeys and seed for the birds, and my dad would give me some money for this; then I ran ahead to the cages. He knew the pattern and would always find me, although one day he probably wished he had not. As he tells it, I had run into the elephant house, where a male elephant stood relieving himself before a silent, somewhat embarrassed crowd of about 30 people. I thought this to be enormously funny, and laughed uproariously, slapping my knees and pointing to the seemingly never-ending fountain. Soon one or two of the adults in the crowd also began to laugh, undoubtedly at my antics, and before long the whole audience was roaring with laughter. When my father came upon the scene, he found, in his words, 'thirty people in a concert of laughter conducted by my four-year-old son'.

Later, when we were forced to leave the Rotterdam area, I missed the zoo as much as anything we left behind. But by then my father had conveyed his fascination with animals (especially birds) and their behaviour, wild and domestic. Many years hence, when the family emigrated to Africa and we made our first of many safaris, I remembered many of the lessons I had learned, in these early years, at my father's side.

My mother was not only a sublime artist but also the ultimate urban explorer, and she took me with her, on the back of her bike, on foot, on bus and tram, whenever she could. She found small markets in isolated neighbourhoods; she knew short cuts to the waterfront, where we sat for hours, watching the world's busiest water traffic on the River Maas. She had an extensive social network, and what a set of characters I met: painters, writers, singers, poets, philosophers. I remember the smells of their ateliers and offices, the long afternoon discussions in stuffy surroundings, the readings and impromptu music-making. I liked only the music, but it was better than being left at home.

My parents were sufficiently well off to be able to have domestic help in the household. Her name was Greetje, and she was an important person in my early life. She was young, cheerful, and always ready for a game, and my parents were obviously fond of her. She was always with me when they were away. I enjoyed her company, and liked being in the kitchen with her while she prepared dinner. While my mother was teaching her last student of the day, Greetje would set the table; after serving us our meal she would eat something in the kitchen and then go home. I thought of her as a member of the family.

In the spring of 1940 I sensed a change in the atmosphere around the house. There seemed to be less music; my father often appeared to be preoccupied and my mother quiet and worried. One afternoon when the weather was good my dad had taken me to a favourite spot along the river to watch the boat traffic and to see if the fishermen had caught anything of interest. As we sat on the embankment, a small flotilla of grey, fast-moving boats appeared. Each had a gun on its bow and a number painted on its side. They looked as though they were in a race, and I noticed that all of a sudden the usual traffic on the river had disappeared. Then, with the boats still in sight, there was a sound of approaching aeroplanes. I thought all this to be very exciting, but my father got his bike, told me to get on the carrier seat, and pedalled off and away from the river as fast as he could. I wasn't sure just why we left so hurriedly, but it was obvious that he had seen something that alarmed him.

The next time I asked to go to the river, my father said we had better not, for a while. That outing turned out to be the last of its kind, but I never knew why. In fact, my parents were spending more time at home than usual, as though they were reluctant to be away at all.

That incident, of which I have such vivid recollection, was the only one prior to 10 May 1940 that interrupted the routine of daily life through that winter and spring. But the Second World War had started nine months earlier, and while the ground fighting went on in Poland, warplanes crossed Dutch airspace. My father knew the risk of being out in the open under an air skirmish. But for the time being, he must have felt that he had been correct in anticipating Dutch neutrality in a wider conflict. At the dinner table there was much talk about the Russians, and how war between Nazi Germany and communist Russia was inevitable.

As the spring progressed, I noticed that my mother's sister, Jeanne Erwich, visited us less often then usual. She lived in Rotterdam, and was my favourite, a lively, widely-travelled, multilingual woman who worked for Unilever, a large company. Her house on the Nieuwe Binnenweg overlooked some of Rotterdam's busiest traffic, and I loved our visits there. When she came to visit us, it always was a festive time. She was well connected in Rotterdam and always had many stories, and brought me books and sometimes a notepad from the company. Not being able to pronounce her French name, I called her 'Sja', which stuck with her for life.

Sja's birthday was on 11 May and was always celebrated in our house. But during the week before her birthday in 1940, she was sombre and downcast. '*Ik heb slecht nieuws*' (I have bad news), I remember her saying to my dad as he helped her with her coat. My father told me to go upstairs, and I assumed that these were matters for adults to discuss. Later I realized what her bad news had been. Through her contacts in Rotterdam she had information about German intentions toward Holland. There would be no Dutch neutrality.

Obviously Sja's news was spreading fast. In our neighbourhood, people began putting up strips of tape across their windows in various patterns – squares, rectangles, diagonals, circles. And in every street, the entrance to a cellar below a public building (a school in our street, the post office across the park) was surrounded by piles of bricks and sandbags. Signs with large arrows appeared along the roads. And from time to time the air was pierced by sounds I had never heard before: the wail of sirens that went up and down like giant trombones. My father explained that they were just practising for now; but some day, when we heard the up-and-down wail, we might have to go to the cellar of the school down the street. There we would wait for the straight sound, a single, long tone, and we would be able to go home.

That seemed pretty exciting to me, and I hoped it would happen soon, because there was not much else to do now. I was not allowed to go out in the street, even on warm, sunny days. My father was home most of the time, but the musicians and students had stopped coming. My mother seemed to be practising exercises on her piano more than she played sonatas, and I sensed a nervous intensity I had never heard before.

On the morning of 10 May, a squadron of German warplanes came overhead but did not, as had been routine in previous weeks, pass over. They circled, and were challenged by Dutch and British fighters. We were sitting at the breakfast table, and my father said to my mother in English, so I would not understand him, 'It is war.' But I understood him well enough, and I remembered Sja's words. Something serious was happening.

The firefight over our town continued and intensified. I had seen just a few planes in my life before, but now the sky seemed filled with them. There was a continuous drone in the air, punctuated by thuds and crackling sounds. Now the sirens were blaring, and you could hear glass breaking.

The rush for the bomb shelters was on. We ran downstairs and opened our front door, but had trouble pushing out into the throng. It was chaos: some people were running towards the shelter entrance, but others were headed the other way and bumped into them. People fell, got up again, and kept running. My father told us to move as close to the wall as possible as we ran. Fortunately

14

we did not have far to go. In our street at least, no one seemed to be hurt by shrapnel or falling glass.

The bomb shelter was so crowded that many people were standing, and the whole cellar was illuminated by only a few bare light bulbs, giving the scene an eerie, ghostlike cast. The brightest spot was the entrance, despite the bricks and sandbags. More people kept arriving, some carrying a few belongings. It was, I thought, amazingly quiet for so many people. Half a dozen in our house made more noise than this large crowd.

Outside, the sounds of war rose and fell, only to rise again; a lull obviously did not mean the end of whatever battle was going on. The air in the cellar became stale, then stifling; some people moved to the entrance, even went outside when it was quiet. But my father told us to stay well inside until the siren sounded its safe signal. When it did, and we climbed up the steps, I realized that there was nothing pleasant about a session in an air-raid shelter.

3

WAR

The aerial dogfight that sent us running to the bomb shelter signified the inevitable: the Netherlands had been attacked and invaded by Nazi Germany. News of the onslaught was on the radio; Germany was demanding immediate capitulation. Traffic on the Lange Nieuwstraat dwindled to just a few vehicles, but pedestrians, many in panic, took over part of the street as well as the pavement. People carried bundles and packages, suitcases and boxes. Shops were jammed, their supplies soon exhausted. There was news that the royal family was fleeing to England, and that people were boarding boats to escape across the North Sea.

There was also news that the small Dutch Army was putting up a heroic fight against the overwhelming German ground forces. I heard one locale mentioned time and again: the Grebbeberg, a hill near the Dutch–German border where the Hollanders were stopping the German incursion and thwarting the Nazis' offensive. Meanwhile, warplanes were overhead every day, and the sirens kept going on and off. From my window I saw that the number of people rushing to the shelters diminished by the day, and that there were some people on the street even after the warning signal had started. My father decided that we would stay in the house. The biggest danger was shrapnel and falling glass, and running down the street entailed more risk than hiding in the windowless anteroom next to the music room. So that is what we did. Life at home continued in a strange new routine: meals at the usual times, but interruptions at any time. From my parents' conversation I could tell the foreboding. My father said that he expected the Germans

16

in the streets of Rotterdam at any hour. My mother wondered how long our food supply would last.

And then, on the morning of 14 May 1940, all our lives changed for ever amid the deafening roar of warplanes, the scary staccato of machine-guns, the thunderous explosions of bombs. Before the day was out, the glow of raging fires and the smell of acrid smoke transformed the small world I knew into something incomprehensible, frightening, overwhelming. What I did not know was that the Germans, frustrated by the defending forces of the Netherlands, had decided to destroy the city of Rotterdam to secure Dutch capitulation. For hours on end, bombers dropped explosives on the city while fighter planes strafed the streets. Before long, Rotterdam's centuries-old inner city was transformed into a hell of fire. Civilians by the hundreds died under collapsing buildings and in death-trap bomb shelters. Errant bombs fell randomly on neighbourhoods throughout the city. Burning planes hit by anti-aircraft fire crashed into houses and streets. Crowds panicked and ran in search of safety; others tried to hook up fire-fighting equipment to douse the flames.

By evening, the sky over the city was as red as a vivid sunset. The roof of our house had a skylight situated in such a way that you could see the skyline of Rotterdam, and even some of the cranes on the docks of its Maas River port. My dad had rigged up a ladder so that you could peer out. When the sounds of war subsided, we went upstairs to see what we could. My mother was angry and called it irresponsible, but my father always had an adventurous streak, and the hours hiding in the ante-room had made him impatient to know what was happening.

What we saw was the city still on fire, occasional explosions brightening the sky like bolts of lightning. Amid the smoke we could see a church tower still standing, silhouetted against a backdrop of crimson. What we could not see was what was happening in the streets: Nazi paratroopers were shooting citizens trying to put out the flames. The city would be left to burn as a lesson to a Dutch government unwilling to capitulate.

The bombardment of Rotterdam was intended to break Dutch resistance against the Nazi invasion. For four days, outnumbered Dutch forces had held up the German advance. The destruction of

Rotterdam, if necessary soon to be followed by the devastation of Amsterdam, would ensure quick capitulation. It did. The Nazi occupation of Holland began during the night of 14 May 1940 and would not end until their surrender to Allied forces on 8 May 1945. I could not realize it then, but on that day the Germans destroyed not only the heart of the city I was learning to love but also the fabric of the country I would shortly come to know. They also destroyed my parents' careers and stole my childhood. These, of course, were minor inconveniences compared to what happened to so many others, including those caught in the raid on Rotterdam. But for those who survived, life would never be the same.

In later years I often wondered why the Allied attack on Dresden in 1945, enacted to break the morale of the Nazi regime and to hasten the end of the war, has become the subject of so much soul-searching and recrimination, while the ravaging of Rotterdam seems, comparatively, to have been forgotten. It is, I suppose, a reflection of the power of post-war Germany in Europe, and its capacity to nudge the world to the notion that the Second World War was just another European conflict in which all sides committed atrocities.

My first five years had been idyllic; the next five would be a time of denial and survival. Survival would become a challenge later; denial began immediately. I suppose that denial is one way children confront, and overcome, what they cannot absorb. That was certainly true in my case. While I sensed the seriousness of what was happening, I remember thinking that there also was something unreal about it all. Standing on that ladder, I could see huge fires raging and great columns of smoke rising into the blaze-lit sky, but I was sure that my mother and I would walk those streets again. It would all come out well.

The days that followed held more of that sense of unreality. Briefly there was some lingering resistance to the Nazi occupations, and occasional skirmishes as Dutch citizens fired on the German occupiers from windows and street corners. From my window seat I was witness to such an attack: a German soldier

18

who stood next to one of the oak trees across from our house, wearing a long green coat and tall black boots, a helmet and leather gloves, suddenly fell to the ground. He never moved, and I was sure that he had just collapsed, as I had seen happen to some of the horses at the warehouse. Later, he was gone. He must have gone on his way, I thought, and I did not connect the commotion that followed – the swarm of Nazi troops, the armoured vehicles and drawn guns – to what I had seen.

What *was* real was that our house no longer resonated with music. My parents were quiet, sombre, obviously worried. About a week after the destruction of the city, things at home seemed especially bleak. Sja had just left, venturing to the city, not knowing whether her house and belongings had survived or were in ruins. But I knew that this was not the whole reason why my mother was in tears and inconsolable. My father, who rarely showed emotion, was tight-lipped and unreachable. I sat in the music room, that room of all the joy, trying to accommodate the new atmosphere of gloom and worry. Only much later did I learn what happened that day. My father had gone out to see how his friends and colleagues had fared. He had found that the cellist of his quartet, who was Jewish, had committed suicide upon the arrival of the Nazi troops.

As the days wore on, my mother's concern over Sja's fate grew. For us, daily life was now confined to our street and part of the park across from the house, as was the case for tens of thousands of other families living in the city in the aftermath of the German assault. My parents assumed that Sja was in the same situation, but not hearing from her was a daily worry.

Finally my mother decided that she would walk to Sja's neighbourhood on the Nieuwe Binnenweg, whether it was sensible to do so or not. I did not realize that she had not told my father about it, but she left him a note and took me with her. Under the best of circumstances such a trek would have taken several hours one way, but on this grey and overcast day it was to be an adventure which is still vivid in my memory.

19

It felt strange walking not just down our street, but taking the turning past the park at the end of it. The bricks and sandbags of the bomb shelter still had not been taken away, and many windows still were taped, but otherwise things seemed normal. We had the pavement almost to ourselves; I had never seen our street, or any other for that matter, with so few people about. After taking the turning I saw one of Rotterdam's familiar yellow trams standing abandoned, some of its glass broken and several holes in one side, but still on the rails. As we walked on, there were some homes with broken windows and some bullet holes in doors and shutters, but looking down side streets the sights were familiar and as I remembered them. It was just so quiet! Where were all the people? I kept wondering.

In 1940, there still was a good deal of open space between Schiedam and Rotterdam, even though Schiedam in reality was a Rotterdam suburb. A major road, flanked by the tramway, crossed several kilometres of what is today a continuous conurbation. As everywhere in Holland, there was a bicycle path beside the road, with a smoother surface and more convenient than the pavement. Since there was almost no bike traffic we walked in the path, and moved along quite quickly. But before long the landscape changed. We could see from a distance a cluster of mounds, several of them, it seemed, right on our route. And to the left and right of the road the ground appeared to have been churned up by some giant machine that left gaping holes and high ridges. I was looking at the first bomb craters of the war in Holland, and several of the bombers had scored direct hits on the road and the tramway. The craters themselves were filled with water; cobblestones lay scattered, like gravel, all over the place. My mother said something about our good fortune that the dikes had not been breached by bombing, but I could see that it would be easy to drown in one of those clay-ringed holes filled with that black water. We clambered around the various obstacles in our way and continued where the bike path resumed.

As we approached the perimeter of Rotterdam, we could see some of the impact of the bombardment, still just weeks ago. The German attack had focused on the city centre, but errant bombs and downed planes had struck the outskirts as well. Now we passed burned-out houses and apartments, piles of rubble, and buildings with not just some, but all of their windows blown out. Soon my mother began to recognize landmarks destroyed by the bombing, and the house of an acquaintance burned out and with no signs of life. We had to watch out for shards of glass, bricks, and other rubble on the pavement. We had been lucky in Schiedam, I realized.

As we walked along the road that led to the Nieuwe Binnenweg, we could see how badly shops and businesses had fared in the attack of 14 May. As in Schiedam, some shops were open again, and shopkeepers stood at the doors; but there had been no deliveries, there was no food for sale, and no one was buying anything else. One shopkeeper told us that the Nazi authorities had organized a food market at an intersection nearby, but that you could buy only basics such as bread and flour.

Larger stores had fared no better. As we neared the Nieuwe Binnenweg we passed a block-long department store that had been badly damaged, probably by the bomb that had made a hole in the middle of the road next to it. Almost all the huge plate-glass windows facing the street had been shattered, and the pieces still lay on the pavement and in the road. We walked carefully, keeping our eyes to the ground. About halfway down the block we saw an unusual sight: one of the enormous store windows had a hole about 2 metres across, right in the middle. The hole was nearly perfectly circular. Pieces of the glass lay among the goods in the display case, still intact and still untouched. We stopped to look, and my mother said that it seemed as though someone had punched that hole with a hammer.

At that instant, with hardly any noise and no warning, what remained of the pane of glass fell towards us. I instinctively grabbed my mother, expecting to be hit. My mother bent over. But all we felt was a rush of air. The pane smashed onto the pavement with a loud crash, glass flying everywhere – and left us untouched. The hole in the centre had passed over us, a perfect fit. Not even our ankles were cut. It was a miracle; had we stopped half a metre in either direction, we would have been hit by the weight of centimetre-thick glass and cut, or worse.

Shaken, we continued, seeing down side streets ugly gaps in

block-long facades where houses had collapsed or burned. But from a distance we could see that the area of my aunt's house was undamaged, a great relief. Our step quickened. Then, when we were about 200 metres from her door, the air suddenly was pierced by the rattle of an aeroplane engine. It got so close so suddenly that we hardly had time to react; the plane seemed to come right down the street, right at us. It was the start of a low-level dogfight between British and German planes, right above us, right over the area where we were walking. Bullets and shrapnel flew everywhere; the noise was so deafening that we could not communicate. One plane, I was sure, passed between, not above the buildings down the street, pursued by another, flying higher and firing downwards at it. We ran frantically to the entrance of my aunt's house, where my mother pushed me between herself and the door, pushing and pulling the manual doorbell. Across the street, glass and brick shattered under a row of bullets. We were the only people still outside. But inside, no one could open the door. My mother pushed so hard against it that the handle could not be pulled back. Presently the gunfire abated, and my mother momentarily leaned back to look down the street. At that moment, the door opened, and we fell inside. Jeanne was nearly hysterical. My mother, unaware why the door had not been opened to us, was beside herself, frantic from fear.

But at least Sja was alive and reasonably well. Her house had suffered little damage; one block away a whole row of homes had burned to the ground. Sitting at the window of her living room, I wondered why so many more people were walking and bicycling around here than in Schiedam, where the damage was so much less. I did not realize that food, in the inner city, was harder to find than in our smaller town. 'I walked to the riverfront to see if any barges had arrived with anything to eat, just this morning,' Sja said. 'That's what all those people are doing. Looking for food.'

The long walk back left me with memories of a dying city: piles of rubble, shells of homes, mounds of garbage, the stench of rot and decay. And it would be years before I realized that I had not seen anything like the worst of it. Rotterdam's historic district was gone, the city's heart torn out. And its five-year nightmare had only just begun.

22

My gentle life in a sunny, music-filled, secure and stable home now was a fast-fading memory. My parents tried to re-establish a semblance of routine, practising in the mornings, working on duos in the afternoons. But I knew their music well enough to realize that this was work, not pleasure; exercise, not art. It was summer now, and I longed for those outings that used to come with the long, warm days of the season. But I knew that this was a time to keep to myself, and not to cause trouble, of which there was obviously enough already. It was amazing that so sombre an atmosphere could envelop a house with such sun-filled rooms and so many cheerful melodies.

Our neighbourhood, too, took on a new ambience. The busy Lange Nieuwstraat remained quiet, almost traffic-less. The large doors of the warehouse remained shut and locked. The port lay silent. I missed the clop-clop of the horses, the rattle of the iron wagonwheels on the cobblestones of the street, the shouts of the vendors, the blasts of ships' horns. On the pavements, German soldiers in green uniforms patrolled. The bearded old patriarch of the Jewish family living two doors away, who always took a morning walk in the park, now wore a large yellow star on his overcoat. I thought he looked more bent over than usual, and soon I saw him there no longer. At the park's entrances, workmen erected signs saying *Voor Joden Verboden*, forbidden for Jews. It was the beginning of a horror whose proportions were then not yet imagined.

And still, somehow, wartime life took on a certain rhythm. It was summer, and farm produce arrived in those stores that reopened. Mail delivery resumed. The fighting had moved elsewhere, and the Nazis began to allow some removal of rubble. Roads were repaired, and people ventured farther afield on their bikes. Newspapers reappeared, their contents controlled by German censors. On the radio, news announcers described German successes in France and the imminent collapse of Britain. Sometimes our street was cleared for marching, singing battalions of German soldiers to pass on their way to Rotterdam. One of their endlessly repeated songs ended with the rhythmic phrase *Und Wir Fahren Gegen Engeland* (and we drive against England). Dutch kids following the column would keep the beat going by singing *plons, plons* (splash, splash).

23

My parents' worries were compounded by financial problems, and talk of war and money dominated dinner-table conversation. The Rotterdam Philharmonic Orchestra obviously would not have a 1940–41 season; Jewish members were ousted, a number of musicians had died in the 14 May bombardment, and its performance hall was destroyed in the bombing and subsequent fires. My mother's teaching practice also suffered, and the family's income declined sharply. One evening my father said that we might have to leave Schiedam if things did not improve.

At least the messages from Sja were less pessimistic. The Nazis had taken control of Unilever, the large firm for which she worked as personal secretary to the director, but operations continued and so far no one had been dismissed. She would continue to receive a salary. She felt fortunate to be fluent in German at a time when that might be a matter of financial survival.

But as the autumn days shortened and the bleak Dutch winter approached, hope seemed to dim. Shortages of firewood, coal, and occasionally food revealed the weakness of the new order. Everyone we knew tried to make the best of it, especially on 5 December, Santa Claus Day, when the children of Holland get presents for having been good the previous year. *Sinter Klaas* would arrive by ship from Spain accompanied by *Zwarte Piet* (Black Pete), his faithful (and fearful) assistant. In his large jute bag, Piet had toys for the good kids, and a stick for those who had been bad. Santas would hold court in town squares and shopping streets, and crowds of youngsters lined up to find out whether they had been good enough to merit a reward. Those festivities were cancelled by the circumstances, but the tradition was not, and countless thousands of mothers made bright red, white-trimmed costumes for fathers to play Santa in. Santa visited my house just after my father had said that he had to go to a concert. His floppy hat hung over his face and his white beard hung by an elastic band, but I was convinced – and terrified when he somehow seemed to know of a misdeed or two. Out of the jute bag (Piet was waiting downstairs) came a tramcar! After Santa left, my mother asked what I thought of him. 'He walks just like dad,' I am reported to have replied.

My father had built that tramcar in painstaking detail in his workshop, where he also fashioned reeds for his 'infernal' oboe. Toys were almost impossible to get, but Santa came and brought something to every family we knew. It was a bright moment in dark times,but nothing similar could lift the gloom of Christmas and New Year. New Year's Eve was the only night of the year I was allowed to stay up until midnight, and when the clock struck 12, my mother served a light meal. As my dad laid his napkin on his lap, he said that this would be the last New Year in this house. My mother did not argue. She knew that we could not survive on what was left of their careers.

4

MOVING

The grim, unusually cold winter of 1941 seemed to worsen the harshness of the Nazi occupation. The German authorities imposed ever stricter controls over the citizens of Rotterdam and its environs, and some elected officials were replaced by Hollanders who sympathized with Nazi objectives. For the first time I heard my parents discuss an organization called the NSB, the National Socialist Union. Members of the NSB not only served in the police force and in city administration; they also informed on their Dutch neighbours. They were dangerous; as you did not know who, among your friends and neighbours, might belong to the NSB, you had to be careful. I wondered who, among the artists and musicians who had so often visited us, might possibly support the Nazi cause. I could think of no one. But my father told me not to answer any questions about our daily life or that of our friends. And if anyone asked me such questions, I was to tell him.

The signs of the new order were everywhere. The Dutch flag had disappeared and displaying it was a serious offence. Mention of the names of any of the members of the Dutch royal family was forbidden. All street names referring to the House of Orange were replaced. When people wore orange flowers on anniversary days such as the Queen's birthday, this was quickly prohibited, and defying the order meant jail. Germans in or out of uniform could demand entry into any dwelling, office, school, or church. All privacy was essentially abolished. It was 1984 in 1941.

There was no reason to believe that things were better anywhere

26

else, but it was clear that we would have to leave. Cultural life in the Rotterdam area was dying, and artists seemed to be particular targets of the Nazi authorities, perhaps because many were Jewish. An NSB member who knew that you had Jewish friends would report that without fail. Our house on the Lange Nieuwstraat had been a wonderful refuge from what was happening all around, and my mother could not bear the thought of leaving it, but there was no choice. My father asked his colleagues and friends to let him know of any opportunities for musicians anywhere else in the country, but of course most of them were looking too.

In the spring he heard of a position that would soon become open in a radio orchestra in the town of Hilversum. This town, located in the Province of Utrecht, had become the centre of Dutch radio stations, and the largest of these organizations had their own orchestras. My father strapped his violin to his bicycle and rode the 40 kilometres or so to Hilversum, requested an audition, and was offered the job on the spot.

That same day he was made aware, however, that housing in the Hilversum area would be a problem. This was the communications centre of the Netherlands, and the Germans had taken over all available accommodation. When he got back home, my parents weighed the options. It seemed to be a secure position, in so far as anything was secure under the occupation. The wages were good, and opportunities for additional work were available. But there was the question of residence. My mother said that she would want to live in a house comparable to the one in Schiedam – but where, if not in Hilversum? As it happened, a family friend who was a prominent physician owned an estate in the Province of Utrecht, not far from Hilversum. He invited us to stay in his guest house, and my parents set out on a tandem to search for a place to live.

A comparatively large town, Hilversum was surrounded by several smaller villages in almost all directions. But even there, housing was hard to come by. The German presence in strategically important Hilversum had spread into its environs, so nearby villages also were crowded. After several days of exploration, my father found an available house in a village named Soestdijk, about 12 kilometres from Hilversum. By Dutch standards that was a long way from work, but there was a good road between village and town, and good bicycle paths as well. They rented the house there and then, and the next day we were on our way back to Schiedam.

The next evening we sat at the dining-room table as my father described the village to which we would be moving. He opened an atlas to show me where Soestdijk was located relative to Schiedam and Rotterdam. I noticed that, on the map, the letter size for Soestdijk was tiny compared to the big black print used to show the location of Rotterdam. Soestdijk was in another province, and in that province the big city was Utrecht; all roads seemed to converge on it. There was a railway line from Utrecht past Soestdijk to a somewhat larger town called Baarn, but no rail link between Soestdijk and Hilversum. My dad would have to bike back and forth.

The map fascinated me. I had never looked at such a map for practical reasons; I had never expected to live anywhere else but Schiedam. Now we would live closer to Amsterdam than to Rotterdam, closer to the Ijssel Lake than to the North Sea. I could find no major river or port anywhere near Soestdijk, but our outings to the Maas River had stopped long ago anyway, and the port behind us remained largely idle. I asked about our street in the village. Was it busy? I loved to sit at our second-floor window and watch the people and traffic; what would substitute for that in Soestdijk? My father said that our street was pretty quiet, but 100 metres away there was that main road from Amsterdam, and it was busier than our street. But can you see it from the house? I wanted to know. Soestdijk looked like a step down to me. And how could you not live on or near the water?

The very next day the preparations for departure began, an unsettling time as chaos seemed to take over. Carpets and paintings were wrapped, dishes packed until there were just enough left for the three of us to use. How different the house looked, how bare and sad! I wondered if it would miss all those musical sounds, the practising, the lessons and performing. I sat one last time in my favourite spot at the window, and resolved to come back to visit as soon as I could. That took rather longer than I anticipated: 50 years.

Soestdijk proved to be not just any Dutch village. On its western edge, no more than 800 metres from our new house, lay the royal family's summer home, *Paleis* (Palace) Soestdijk. Surrounding the palace were extensive forests known as the Crown Domain, parts of which were open to the public. Huge fir, oak and beech trees gave the woods a quiet, imposing character. The major road from Amsterdam cut through these forests, passed in front of the palace, and continued through the heart of the village. Where that road made a sharp bend was the village centre, dominated by a stately inn known as the Viersprong. Our house was just up a side street from the inn.

My impression of Soestdijk's remoteness, gleaned from the atlas map, seemed to be correct. Yes, the road from Amsterdam was busy, but few cars or trucks slowed down or stopped as they passed through the village. Next to the Viersprong was a garage, complete with petrol pumps, and some activity went on there. But the whole inside part of the bend in the road was taken up by a large convent and a Catholic church, not, I figured, the kinds of enterprises to stimulate traffic and daily interaction. But, as the months and years ahead would prove, Soestdijk's remoteness had its advantages during war and occupation. Some of the harshest rules and regulations imposed by the Nazis on the larger cities and towns took time to take effect here.

When we arrived, the Nazis had not yet ordered changes in all street signs that carried the names of members of the royal family. Our new address was Julianalaan (Juliana Lane) 1, at the intersection of Wilhelminalaan. (Wilhelmina was Queen of the Netherlands, and Juliana was her daughter.) Before long, however, the Nazi edict took effect in Soestdijk, and our street became Louise de Coligny Lane. It wasn't easy to pronounce. I never tried to find out who Louise de Coligny was; if she was acceptable to the Nazis, she would be of no interest to me.

Our village house was a free-standing home with front, side and back gardens. Big oak trees stood in front, fruit trees at the back. A huge walnut tree towered over the area between us and our neighbours. Berry bushes grew everywhere. The garden was rather unkempt, ideal, I thought, for running and playing. I remember the fragrance of that back garden, the budding and blossoming apple and pear trees. There was a shed for tools, firewood and garden equipment, and my parents said that we would be working quite hard on the grounds. Across the street, the triangular lot where the Juliana and Wilhelmina Lanes intersected had been made into a small park filled with flowers.

To me the house seemed wonderfully spacious, with three bedrooms on the second floor and the fourth in the partially finished attic upstairs. Moreover, I had my own room and it was at the front, overlooking the street and the small park. The music room was right next to mine, complete with grand piano; the other grand, a Berdux and my mother's favourite, was in the living room downstairs. Beneath the kitchen was a small basement, where in years to come my mother would store countless bottles of preserved fruits and cardboard containers filled with walnuts. Four years hence, this harvest would help save our lives.

The Dutch, in general, are a gregarious people who welcome new neighbours graciously and open-heartedly. But this was a time of uncertainty, and therefore caution. An NSB family in the neighbourhood could spell danger, even disaster; and no one knew the background of the de Blijs, the new arrivals at Julianalaan 1. So getting to know the neighbours took some time. To our left, up the street, was an older couple, Mr and Mrs Richter. He was an amateur carpenter who made garden chairs, benches, tables – his garden was filled with them. He had a workshop with every imaginable tool, and the sounds of sawing and hammering could be heard almost every day. To the right lived two ladies in their seventies, the 'Ladies Bakker' as we called them. And across the intersection with the Wilhelminalaan, beyond the little park, lived a family we would come to know intimately, the Batenburgs. They had nine children ranging in age from four to twenty-five. The two youngest, Bernard and Paul, were the first to talk to me in the street; they became close friends. The head of the family, a short, bald-headed man with an intense face, held an important position in the village: he was secretary of the village council. In the terror that lay ahead, his advance warnings to my father of Nazi raids on our neighbourhood would ensure our survival.

Life in the village was nothing like that in Schiedam. Our brick-paved street was as quiet as the Lange Nieuwstraat had been bustling. A few bicycles, an occasional horse-drawn wagon, a car now and then, some people on the pavement carrying groceries, but that was all. Even the busy main road from Amsterdam, past the Viersprong, could not match the city. Our village did have something the Schiedam area did not, however: sloping ground. Living in the delta of the Maas River, I had never seen mountains or even hills, but the Wilhelminalaan (as we still called it) rose from the Batenburgs' home upwards to a hill grandiosely called the Lazarusberg. In Dutch, *berg* means mountain, and I had seen mountains in pictures, and this was no mountain, I thought. Lazarus*heuvel* (hill) would have been more appropriate. But the slope was steep enough so that boys on bikes raced downhill at breakneck speed. In the winter, Bernard and Paul told me, there was great sledging on the Lazarusberg.

One evening at dinner I told my parents that I had walked to the top of the Lazarusberg, and that you could see over much of the village from there. My father said that the 'mountain' had been built by glaciers. That was why there were some big boulders on the slope: the ice had pushed it all into a mound. That was amazing. I wondered what made the ice disappear.

Apart from the military traffic on the Amsterdam road, I saw far fewer German soldiers in Soestdijk than in Schiedam. But the fearful regulations imposed by the Nazis affected our village too. I heard my parents talk about them: even before we arrived, all Jews were compelled to register with the village council. The mayor, we were told, was doing a heroic and dangerous job of expunging records and deferring the registration of Jews in mixed marriages. Still posted publicly was an order dated 20 June 1941 prohibiting Jews from renting rooms in public lodgings. Another order informed citizens that all correspondence with the town hall would henceforth have to be written in German, and that correspondence in Dutch would be discarded. That was frightening: most people in the village probably knew little or no German. Mr Batenburg told us not to worry. 'They'll never be able to police that,' he said.

A more immediate concern was food. My father was earning a

good income, but food was in short supply and money made no difference. Even before we arrived in the village, rationing ('distribution', as the Nazis called it) had started. There were coupons for everything, from basics such as bread and potatoes to milk and vegetables. Coupons were also needed for such things as soap and bicycle tyres. But what the coupons yielded was an inadequate diet and too little sustenance. Greetje, the loyal maid, had come with us to Soestdijk from Schiedam, but my parents could not provide her enough food. After eight difficult months she returned to the city, a tearful farewell; would we ever see each other again? She said that she would look after Sja if circumstances permitted. As it turned out, she and Sja survived the war in Rotterdam.

My father's commute to and from Hilversum was eased by the coincidence of our location: our garden backed up to a shed behind the garage on the Viersprong, and he got to know the owner. Thus, for a few months, my dad was able to get a few precious litres of petrol, and he would set out in the morning, dressed in his leather coat and with his violin strapped across his chest, to the studio. Before long he was playing solo parts and we were able to hear him on the radio. But things would soon change. In the late summer of 1941 an order required all citizens to yield to the authorities any and all items made of metal, including everything from birdcages to chandeliers and from kitchen utensils to garden tools. Vehicles were not specifically mentioned, but soon Germans were taking bicycles from their owners right in the street. My dad realized that his Royal Enfield would be confiscated, but he was not prepared to give it up. So he hid it in our garage under a pile of wood and rags, and began his commute by bicycle in the hope that his identity papers might prove his need for it.

The regulation compelling all citizens to carry identity papers issued by the Nazis was especially frightening. Each 'legitimization' document, as it was called, had one's picture, age, address, job and other data; any special permissions were also recorded. My dad's papers, for example, explained his being on the road late, after performances. But all these documents had a time limit. They had to be renewed, and if anything changed, permissions would be withdrawn. My father, in his mid-thirties in 1941, was especially vulnerable: men his age were beginning to be rounded up for labour gangs. But as long as he held his orchestra post, he gathered, his chances were good.

Soestdijk had no suitable public school, my parents decided, so one autumn morning in 1941 my mother took me on her bicycle to the village of Baarn to register at the Nieuwe Baarnse School, a small, private elementary school located in a residential area. To get there, you biked past the palace and through the Crown Domain along the Amsterdam road; at the first big intersection you turned right (left if you wanted to go to Hilversum). From there the bike path skirted the forest to the right; to the left was a series of magnificent villas. About midway down this road you turned left, crossed the railway line to Amsterdam via a pedestrian bridge, and followed a winding street to the school entrance. It took about a half-hour. 'Well, we still have our bikes,' my mother said when we arrived. The Germans at this point were taking only male bikes, not (yet) those ridden by women or children.

The school building had formerly been a private mansion, converted now to a different function but still showing some of its original grace and elegance. Ceilings were high, rooms large and airy. Tall, wide windows let in ample light. The gardens had been converted into a fenced playground. When we arrived, some children were already out there waiting for the first bell to ring. 'You'll have lots of fun playing with new friends,' my mother said as we waited for my registration to be checked. But I glanced into the rows of desks in the classroom and realised that life was about to take a nasty turn.

I hated being left behind and made a terrible scene. My mother promised to meet me after school but I was inconsolable. It must have been embarrassing, and my teacher, Miss Kort, was not especially sympathetic. And I obviously behaved pretty stupidly. I never seemed to understand instructions or get things right; in that first week I found myself sitting at my desk through the mid-morning break because I had failed to get instructions right and had done some task or other the wrong way. Sitting in that class-

33

room by myself and hearing the sounds of children playing outside made me feel pretty miserable. Feeling far from home did not help. School was not going to be a favourite experience.

Most of all, I had difficulty with the notion that I would be confined to this place much of every day of the week but Sunday. It seemed to be a long way from home, and I'd be surrounded by strangers and under the supervision of someone I did not even know. Pretty scary, I thought, no matter that my parents told me how good a school the Nieuwe Baarnse School was supposed to be.

There were about 20 kids in my first-year class, and our room (all six classes had their own rooms) was on the ground floor. Sliding French doors separated our classroom from that of the second-year class, so you could see what was going on next door. A blackboard extended across the entire front wall of the room, and on the teacher's table stood a huge globe. Maps and pictures lined the other walls. A bookcase overflowed with books. This was going to be a serious experience.

But my idea of fun was going home, and behind the building was a roofed bike rack for students who rode to school. Having a bike would make for a sense of freedom, I was sure. And although I did not yet have a bike, the school did assign me a rack space: number 40. That alone was encouraging. The lower numbers were nearer the exits, and that is where the senior students had their spaces. But I would not mind having to wait a while before being able to leave, so long as I was sure I was leaving.

School days were long: a morning and afternoon session every day except Wednesdays and Saturdays, when there were morning sessions, 9 to 12, only. School started at 9 and let out at 4, so that, when I had my own bike, I would be able to ride home for lunch. From the very first day there was what seemed to me a mountain of homework; every hour produced some work to be done by the next day. Subjects ranged from arithmetic to the arts; the latter consisted of making clay objects and ... knitting. I wasn't much good at arithmetic, was a failure at making clay frogs and butterflies, and hated those knitting needles. The art teacher seemed impatient and I could not stand the smelly attic where the clays and paints were kept. Good days were days without art classes.

Bad days ended in that attic, grandiosely labelled *atelier*. I thought of the ateliers I had seen in Schiedam and Rotterdam, and wondered how such an exalted name could be given to this cheerless space.

My class was about half boys and half girls, and we were all issued the mandatory 'legitimization' card. In our case this was a small, laminated one about the size of a credit card, with a short, light metal chain attached. Miss Kort told us to put it around our necks and *never* to take it off. If we were ever lost, someone would know where we lived.

On my birthday in October 1941 I got my first bike, and now I was able to ride to school by myself. Unfortunately my parents had met the parents of a girl my age living up the street, and since she also biked to my school, they all agreed that we should ride together. Every morning Rita stood outside the house calling me, and I kept hoping that she would go on without me so I could ride fast and catch up with her. But my mother insisted that we start together. However, she stayed at school for lunch and I could go home, and I loved those midday rides through the Crown Domain and past the palace, now occupied by German authorities. Always there were tanks, armoured vehicles, cannon and other equipment to see. Getting home took about a half-hour, so I had a whole hour for lunch at home. On sunny days my mother put my sandwich and milk out in the back garden. I savoured those moments before I had to take off again.

But school had its dark, even dangerous side. During the war, the Nazi collaborating NSB became an informal spy organization. Members often kept a low profile, but kept an eye on their neighbours and reported to the Nazi authorities what they learned. In Soestdijk, Baarn and other places, NSB members identified families of Jewish ancestry and helped the Germans draw up lists of people who would, eventually, be taken from their homes and sent to concentration camps. They also noted unusual circumstances that might be of interest to the Nazis. Not far from our home lived a couple who had taken in and hidden two Jewish neighbours. The home of the Jewish couple soon was broken into by uniformed Germans who stripped it of all their possessions. But the couple could not be found – until an NSB spy across the street noticed that milk and other food taken into the house of the good Samaritans had increased substantially. Putting two and two together, the NSB operative alerted the Nazi authorities, who raided the suspect house. The Jewish couple were found and deported, and their benefactors arrested, their house confiscated.

NSB members used their children to obtain information, which made school a risky place. Children talk about their parents, and often exaggerate their exploits. Many a father lost his freedom (and some their lives) because their kids boasted of their patriotism. Parents tried to identify families whose children might be informants, but they were not always right. In my class there was a girl with a first name that rhymed with NSB, and whose parents were believed to be collaborators. My father warned me never to talk to her, to walk away should she start a conversation. I was careful – but I never knew that a boy, also in my class, was from an NSB family too. I was to discover this more than 50 years later, when I went back to Holland for the commemoration of the end of the war.

My father continued to ride his bicycle to Hilversum. He had to go much farther than I, but his rehearsals started at 10 a.m., so sometimes we would leave together before Rita arrived. Those were wonderful mornings, and I treasured these rides, going slowly so as to make them last longer. The bike path was wide enough for us to ride abreast, so we could talk about school and work. All too soon he had to turn left and I turned right toward Baarn.

One morning, when we were just past the palace, a German officer walked onto the bike path and motioned us to stop. Speaking in German, he told my father to produce his identity paper. Apparently all was in order; the officer nodded, returned the document and waved us along. 'Well, I still have my bike,' my dad said. But I was pretty frightened. You never knew what a Nazi might do.

One Thursday afternoon shortly after my first birthday in Soestdijk, my mother was waiting for me in the kitchen. There was a surprise in the dining room, she said. I opened the door but saw nothing, except a patch of newspapers spread out in a corner. 'Look under the round table,' my mother said. And there, hiding behind the floor-length tablecloth, was a tiny fox-terrier puppy. I stretched out on the floor and reached under the table, and to my surprise she licked my hand, then cuddled against it, shivering all the while. I pulled her out from under and held her against my chest. She looked up at me, big brown eyes in a tiny face, and it was love at first sight. For the next almost eight years we were nearly inseparable.

When my father came home he had a name ready. 'I know about a Scottish dog that was so loyal that after he lost his master he went every day for the rest of his life to the place where they had always met,' he said. 'They put up a statue for him in Edinburgh, their capital. His name was Bobby. Let's call our new dog Bobby.' It did not occur to me to think whether the name Bobby was appropriate for a female. Bobby it was, and from the day she arrived she brought cheer in dark times.

Bobby's markings would be a topic of endless amusement. Her face, from between the ears to the tip of the nose, was divided exactly into a black left and a white right side. She had one black ear and one white. The divide continued to her chest, and one foreleg was all black, the other nearly all white. Her tail was black, except for the tip, which was stark white.

Feeding Bobby in this time of scarcity would be a challenge, but she needed very little now and would never need very much, as her parents were both of small stature, according to my dad. My mother started her on some small pieces of bread soaked in milk, but even the low rim of the dish was a challenge. Bobby was tiny and wobbly, and that night in her bed in the kitchen she cried for her mother. But my parents told me not to go down, as that would lead to bad habits. Bobby would learn to sleep alone, they said.

Bobby turned out to be the most intelligent, self-reliant, loving, fiercely protective animal I have known in my life. She shared, and often made, our joys and softened our sorrows. She revelled in our momentary good times and suffered with us when we all went hungry. She warned us whenever someone came near the house, once giving my father crucial moments to go into hiding during a Nazi raid on our neighbourhood. In the early years of the war we walked her on a leash, but near the end, when we were too weak, and when it was in any case too dangerous, to go out, we let her go to scrounge what she could. I am convinced that she knew that we were desperate. One day in the winter of 1945 she came home carrying, in her mouth, an unbroken egg. She scratched at the kitchen door and laid it on the mat, looking up at my mother. We shared that egg, the four of us. It was the first one we had seen in months, and a large part of our intake that day.

B ut in the autumn of 1941 all that was in the future. For me in Soestdijk, life presented none of the rush of events I had experienced in Schiedam following the Nazi occupation. One day, coming home from school, I saw some workmen putting up signs stating that the movement of Jews in our village was restricted; I remembered how quickly similar signs had gone up in the city. On another day I saw a truck carrying away all the bells from the church next to the convent. They were neatly laid so that the smaller ones fitted into the larger, two rows of a carillon I would never hear again. But the daily routine of schoolgoing and homework went on.

From my parents' conversation, though, I realized that our village could be a dangerous place under Nazi occupation. Several village officials, some of them friends of the Batenburgs and including the local Inspector of Police, were arrested by the Nazis and never seen again. Earlier, a group of youngsters had thrown stones and had broken a window of a house occupied by a known NSB family. A German patrol had fired on the fleeing teenagers and killed one of them. The local newspaper, which occasionally contained implied criticism of NSB members, was closed down.

Especially worrisome was the Nazi practice of *vorderen*, that is, the confiscation of things ranging from personal property to entire homes. When the Nazis wanted something, they took it. When what they wanted was space or a good location, they would knock on a homeowner's door, inspect the house and, if they liked what they saw, order the family out. Sometimes the residents would be told to leave certain things behind, for example a piano or a refrigerator. Frequently the unfortunate evictees were given just two hours' notice to clear their premises. When you saw a group of people moving belongings on handcarts down the street, you knew what had happened. About all you could do was lend a hand.

I was awake at night worrying about that. What if there were a knock on the door and we would all be in the street? What about my mother's piano? My schoolbooks? Where would we go? What if it happened while I was away at school? Would I say goodbye to my mother and father and find German soldiers at the door when I came back? What if it happened to the Batenburgs, with all those children?

And then a much more immediate threat arose. Suddenly the very reason for which we had come to the Hilversum area, my father's position in the radio orchestra, was over. I already knew of his independence of spirit, stubbornness and quick temper, but I did not realize how dangerous these traits could be in a situation such as ours. When he came home one Sunday afternoon from a concert that was still under way, my mother knew that something was seriously wrong, and they sat in the living room to talk it over. The German authorities had issued orders that all orchestral concerts should begin with the playing of the German national anthem, '*Deutschland über Alles*' ('Germany above All'). This was the first concert where the anthem would be played, but my father refused. Along with an oboe player, he packed his violin up, rose, and left the stage as the music began. The commotion, including applause in the audience, was heard around the country.

No one arrested or even stopped him as he rode home, but my mother was not so sure that he had not risked his freedom. What about the consequences? 'What about us, your wife and son?' she said to my dad. 'We will lose what security we have had until now!'

'Others are losing much more,' my father replied.

In fact it was my mother who made what my dad did possible without immediate disaster. As she had done in Schiedam, she had built up a large piano-teaching practice, and students came and went by the dozens from morning till night. Her income undoubtedly exceeded my father's, so that financially they would be all right, though no longer comfortable. There was talk that I would have to be taken out of my school, and go to the public school in another village. But my parents' real concern was that the Nazi authorities would come to arrest my father, if not in the next several days, then later. At the very least, he would lose the identity paper that had provided some protection against confiscation. For how long would our relatively normal life continue?

5

TENSION

For a civilian population during war, life swings back and forth between the routine and the absurd, the normal and the bizarre, the secure and the perilous. As a boy in elementary school, I was growing up fast, learning to expect the unexpected, to absorb the occasional panic. The winter of 1942 was harsh and bitterly cold, with deep snow on the Amsterdam road and tough going on the way to and from school. There was no question of biking home for lunch, of which there was less and less anyway. The school building was warm, and at least one of the teachers stayed with pupils who could not walk home for lunch.

We would all gather in the fourth-form room upstairs, the warmest in the building, and the teacher organised mind games. These games were mostly for the older kids, and I could not really participate. But there was one I liked. The teacher used a stopwatch and told us that we had, say, seven minutes to come up with any and all geographic names for places, mountains, seas and other features on the map, beginning with a certain letter. The older kids were much better and faster at this than I was, but I always had one or two nobody else had. When the letter was P and my first entry was Pisa, there were groans and laughs. It was mine alone, for extra points. But sometimes the game got too difficult for me. Landlocked countries, mountains in Asia, lakes. Back home I would look at the old Bos Atlas to check up on some of the names I had heard.

My trips to and from school sometimes got exciting. My father had told me long ago always to head for a ditch if I ever heard gunfire, but that still seemed more adventure talk than real to me. But in winter the trip was long and slow and I did have to take cover a few times when a dogfight broke out overhead. Yet in truth I was more afraid of the school's headmaster than I was of whatever might happen on the road to and from school. Mr van Dijk had a volcanic temper that made my dad's seem mild by comparison. He proved, almost daily, that no physical punishment was needed to reduce a pupil to shivers and tears. When his voice bellowed through the door of his office and could be heard all the way downstairs, we all knew that someone had been caught in some offence, had failed a test, or made a mistake. Whoever it was, he or she was going through hell. Van Dijk's hollering sessions could last as long as 30 minutes, and we always wanted to catch a glimpse of the victim, wondering how we would fare if we were in his or her place.

Van Dijk not only was headmaster but also taught the sixth and final year, and to us in the lower forms it was just unimaginable to have him as a teacher every day. But, we knew, the older boys and girls did survive, so there had to be ways to cope. Many fifth-years, though, dreaded leaving the class of the mild-mannered, soft-spoken Mr Vermeer at the end of the school year.

From time to time our teacher, or the second-form teacher, was prevented from reaching the school, and then our classes were combined. The large sliding glass doors that separated our rooms were pushed back to create one large classroom. I liked that because the second-form teacher had lined the walls with maps large and small, and there was also a big globe on her desk. The second form had a geography hour (we did not) and I enjoyed try- ing to answer the questions. In fact, this seemed to be the only thing I felt I was any good at, although I liked singing in the choir during the music hour in the gym. Otherwise I was not a very good student. My handwriting was terrible, and I was always dripping blobs of dark blue ink on paper and desk.

From the beginning my parents, and especially my mother, took an active part in my schoolwork, and I have always been grateful for that. They helped with my homework and suggested ways I could cope with difficult assignments. They also kept in touch with my teachers. Memorizing was a key part of education in those days, and my mother rehearsed my answers for the next day. In arithmetic, we had to learn the multiplication tables for numbers up to 20, and I had great difficulty with that; but she devised a way of using musical tones to match the numbers to make it easier. I have used her system ever since, I can still do them faster than a computer, and have won a few dollars at parties from doubting Thomases by proving her right.

One advantage of the heavy snow of the 1942 winter was that our school was closed several times for 'snow days'. That meant not only no classes, but also no homework. Then I had the opportunity to try my sledge on the slope of the Lazarusberg, and to mix with other kids from the village. But in truth this was a mixed blessing. Beyond the Lazarusberg lay a much poorer part of Soestdijk, a rough area where your bike might get stolen or kids would throw stones at you as you rode down the street. The fronts of houses there had no gardens, and roadsides were muddy and rutted. Some houses had broken windows. Some of the kids in that area, I was told, did not even go to school. But when it snowed they came to slide down the 'mountain'. Kids that did not have sledges used boards.

I just wanted to sledge on the slope, but it was not that simple. When I walked up the hill, I noticed that the bigger boys controlled the path to the top, and if you did not know any of them, they would not let you pass. Younger kids just did not have a chance up there, so I just went uphill as far as they would let me go, and then rode down. One time I must have gone a bit too far, because a big fellow knocked me to the ground, took my sledge and rode downhill. I ran after him, slipping and sliding in the snow, fearing that this was the last I would see of my sledge. But when he got to the bottom he just left it there and walked back up. Bigger boys taking sledges from smaller ones, I soon discovered, was routine. And the bigger boys tended to come from the other part of town. There was no way I would get friendly with any of them, so I had better lower my expectations of 'snow days.'

I told my father about this, but he had his doubts. It was just that I was new here, he said; in time I would have less trouble. I suggested that he come to see for himself, but he was reluctant to leave the house because of the risk involved. But one day he did come, watching the scene from the garden of friends on the street where, if necessary, he could quickly go inside. When he got home, he was upset by what he had seen. 'This should be a playing field, but it looks more like a battleground,' he told my mother. In truth, some of the atmosphere on the slope reminded me a bit of our school playground, where you also had to know what you could and could not do.

But not everyone from the far side of the Lazarusberg was obnoxious. After Greetje had gone back to Schiedam, my parents had looked around for other help in the household and hired a woman named Arris. She came from one of those dilapidated houses to work at our place every Tuesday and Friday, always arriving by seven in the morning and putting in 12-hour days. Arris was the salt of the earth, rough in appearance, speech, habits – but with a heart as good as gold. She was supportive, protective, devoted to us all. When she realized that we were short of some foods, she began to bring items she was able to get from the farms that adjoined her end of Soestdijk. She admired my mother's energy and my father's courage, looked after me when necessary, and adored Bobby. No matter what the circumstances, Arris was always there on her days. Soon she was also working for the Ladies Bakker next door, and her presence in the neighbourhood was reassuring to us all. When times got worse in the village, her early warnings were invaluable.

My father was now at home almost constantly, because it was unsafe for him to go out and risk inspection. Because of his artistic rebellion he was likely to be subject to arrest at some point, and of course his identification now referred to a job he no longer held. That document would soon expire, but the expiry date was right at the bottom of the page. So my mother, using long scissors, carefully cut that section off. Would any 'Green Police', as the Nazi enforcers were called, recognize that this had been done?

His action, though, had come to the attention of the Dutch resistance, and several members of the underground made contact and offered help. So his circle of acquaintances expanded, and he began to get news of the war our official radio stations were not reporting. From the censored media we heard that German offensives everywhere were succeeding, that Britain would soon fall, that North Africa and the Middle East were being overrun, that the Soviet Union would soon be under German sway from Minsk to Vladivostok. But from the Resistance we heard that things were not quite so rosy for the Nazis. A man whom I only knew as Mr Robert sent frequent messages, and my dad sometimes sent me to his house on the Amsterdam road with a brief note acknowledging them.

In July, the Germans announced another round-up of bicycles; this time they would not simply be confiscated on the street if the village 'voluntarily' made available a total of 166 bikes. By appealing to citizens to offer any second bikes in the household, and by getting dealers to contribute, the total was reached – but the Germans did not collect their tribute. Instead, they preferred to enter houses in the dark of night and search for more. Not until September were the 'contributed' bikes finally taken away.

My father realized that any thorough search of our premises would yield not only his and my mother's bikes, but also his motorcycle, by now an illegal property. But he was not prepared to let the Nazis have the Royal Enfield, and so, at dusk one late summer evening, he began digging a deep hole in the back garden, in the middle of the potato patch we had planted there. Over the next several days the hole got deeper and deeper, with a slope at one end of it. He lined the sides with pieces of plywood and old planks and the floor with sawdust that he had been collecting in the workshop. Finally he wheeled his beloved bike down the slope and into the hole. He smeared a kind of reddish paste all over it, then stuffed oil-soaked rags, pieces of carpet and old newspapers around it. Next, he fashioned a roof about half a metre below the surface, so that there would be enough soil above the bike to grow a row of potatoes right over its oily grave. 'It probably won't survive, but I'd rather let it rust than turn it over to the Nazis,' said my dad as we smoothed the soil and scattered leaves over it.

My mother had her doubts. What if the motorcycle were discovered? People were arrested, but usually released after a time, for hiding their bicycles. But others had been taken away, never to be seen again, for doing less than my dad had just done. My father's obstinacy was dangerous, obviously, in these uncertain times.

I enjoyed my father being home as much as he was, except for one thing: more violin lessons. Now he had time not only to teach me more often but also to monitor my practising. He had given me a quarter-size violin that fitted any size but had very little tone, and I was pretty frustrated at my slow rate of progress. But practising the violin certainly concentrated the mind. Patience was not one of my dad's virtues, and with his capacity for perfect pitch he had little tolerance for out-of-tune playing, which was (and, according to him, has always been) a speciality of mine. Still, it was thrilling to be able to play some of the melodies I had heard my parents perform, and there were moments when these music lessons had their positive side.

Circumstances restricted my social life quite severely. When school was in session, there was no time; upon getting home at 4.30 p.m. I had to start my homework right away or I would not finish by bedtime. Even when there was no school my parents did not want me to go farther away than just across the street. Unexpected things did happen: in the early spring a burning German warplane fell on three houses in the Talma Lane and killed six people. In July a woman at home was severely injured by shrapnel from anti-aircraft guns operating near the village. Several summary executions took place in various parts of Soestdijk. Homes continued to be confiscated at hours' notice. And the Resistance began to harass the German authorities, risking retaliation. It was better to be home, or near home, whenever possible.

I marvel to this day at my parents' ability to create for me a childhood as normal as it was. Only intermittently did I realize how fearful they were, and how difficult it was for them to live with the reality that, for all of us, this life might end at any moment. Fathers had been ripped from their families, families we knew, never to be seen again. Others hid in cellars, attics, even in haystacks on farms. And always there was the threat that my father's actions in Hilversum would come to haunt us.

From the Resistance we learned some reasons why my father had hitherto escaped pursuit. Our village and rural area did not

46

have the kind of stable, continuous Nazi administration larger cities and towns had. The German authorities based in the nearby, larger village of Soest were frequently redeployed, and while the new authorities always seemed even harsher than the ones who had left, the repeated discontinuity abrogated many a trail of pursuit. Also, we learned, the Resistance had been able to infiltrate the administration to steal and destroy civil records (several members had lost their lives in such efforts). Early in 1943 a member of the Resistance brought my father a falsified Nazi document, an identity paper that overstated his age by ten years and removed him from the most dangerous age bracket for forced-labour round-ups. These round-ups, which we called *razzias*, had become a part of life in the village during that winter. They were to become part of the terror of the last two years of the war.

For others, things were far worse than they were for us. In April1 1943 the Nazis proclaimed that it was no longer legal for any Jewish families to reside, or find themselves for any reason, in the Province of Utrecht, our province. Many already had sought refuge with Dutch families, but some Jews walked to the concentration camp at Vught in the hope of escaping deportation. On 28 July 1943 the mayor of Soestdijk was ordered to report the names of any Jews of whom he knew, and suggest any reason to exempt them from deportation. The mayor, whose letter of response hangs in a Soestdijk museum to this day, reported that he knew of only six Jews, all exempt because of intermarriage, none of whose addresses were available to him. A few days later, the underground broke into the town hall and stole the village register. But Jews from other provinces were not so lucky. Soon, an endless column of Dutch Jews, most dressed in black and carrying suitcases and bundles, began to move along the main road from Amsterdam, heading west. Those marches went on for days, then weeks. Villagers who tried to hand the marchers some food or drink were beaten back by Nazis patrolling the route. I asked my parents who the marchers were and where they were going; these were not just young men who could serve as labourers but oldsters, women and children my age as well. My mother put her finger on her lips. There was no answer. Between us, standing on the pavement, and those people walking in the street was a chasm of death.

During my summer vacation in 1943 I became aware of something called the SD, the Nazi security police. The Nazi SD took over many of the functions previously performed by the 'Green Police', and these SD officers were even tougher-looking. They wore leather coats, big black boots, had a large revolver in a very visible holster, and rode on big, loud motorcycles. Unlike the 'Green Police', these SD officers seemed always to move in groups, roaring up and down the village streets and intimidating citizens.

The SD took over the organization and execution of the *razzias*, and Mr Batenburg warned my father that he should now stay in hiding, because the SD had new lists of 'seditious' persons. In truth, I think that my parents had become somewhat lax about his security.

One morning in midsummer I opened the curtains in my room and saw a dozen or more SD officers, machine-guns levelled, on the street and in the little park, looking at our house. I could not believe that I would not have heard their motorcycles, but saw none anywhere. At that moment my mother rushed in, put a coat over my pyjamas, and ran me downstairs and out of the back door, through the hedge and to the far side of the Ladies Bakker's house. 'Walk over to the Batenburgs,' she ordered. I did, realizing that this was real danger; but a small boy like me would go unnoticed crossing the street.

From the window of the Batenburgs' house I saw what happened next. An officer arrived and ordered the policemen to surround our house, and two of them banged on the front door. My mother opened it, and they stepped inside, followed by two or three others. Bobby, our little fox terrier, barked furiously at the Germans; I could hear her even inside Mrs Batenburg's living room. The door closed, but about ten minutes later it opened again, and the Germans came out. Bobby was still barking. My mother closed the door, and my father was nowhere to be seen. Now the SD went over to Mr Richter's house next door, and some went up the street to the next house.

I wondered why the Germans had not taken my dad; I knew he had been at home that night. What I did not know was that he had fashioned a hiding place behind one of the wood-burning stoves that stood in each room of the house. The stove was backed by a heavy black metal plate that fitted against the arched opening for the pipe's elbow. There was enough space for him to crawl into that opening, and he would pull the stove back into position while my mother pushed it. That morning, just before the knock on the door, he had hidden there. Later, when I heard them talking about it, my mother said that she had worried that Bobby might betray the secret, but she had been so noisy that her barking seemed to distract the Nazis.

But I did not learn about my father's hiding place for a very long time. The Germans often interrogated and even tortured children, trying to get them to reveal where their fathers or uncles were. It was better if I really did not know. In any case, I had become used to my dad's irregular presence, and learned never to ask where he was.

I had by then begun to lose the shield of denial and understood the possibility that some disaster might befall us as it did so many of my friends in the village and at school. Mr Batenburg said that he felt that this *razzia* was a general search for able-bodied men to be put to work in German factories and construction sites, but there was the possibility that it started where it did, with our house, before moving up the street, because my father's name had come up on a 'seditious persons' list.

Years after the Second World War ended, my father got evidence that the Nazis' search for him did indeed have the latter motive. By then my parents had decided to emigrate, and this entailed a lengthy exit interview with Dutch authorities involving matters of legal record, taxation and the like. 'Before you depart, Mr de Blij,' said the Dutch official handling his case, 'I think you may want to see this, which is part of your dossier.' It was a letter written by a colleague in my father's orchestra, someone of whose NSB sympathies he had been unaware. The letter described my father as a 'dangerous terrorist' capable of doing 'severe damage' to German objectives in the Netherlands, someone who should be 'eliminated' at the earliest opportunity. My father was dumbfounded; but what was especially painful was that the individual who had written that letter to the Nazi authorities now occupied a good position in a prominent Dutch symphony orchestra.

49

By mid-1943 German war fortunes were turning sour, and among the people of our village hope rose even as repression intensified. There was talk of an invasion, and the Resistance grew ever bolder. The entire village population register was stolen during a night-time raid. Wallposters appeared throughout Soestdijk, urging citizens to 'Resist with the Resistance'. The police station in Soest was overrun and pistols and ammunition stolen.

Nazi retaliation came in several forms. All radio receivers had to be turned in to authorities; if a radio were found in a home during a *razzia*, the owner would be executed. The hours during which citizens could be outside their houses were curtailed. Under so-called *sperrzeit* regulations, you could be shot on sight if you were in the street during prohibited hours. When we arrived in Soestdijk in 1941, the *sperrzeit* was no major problem: it ran from midnight to 4 in the morning. But now the Nazis extended it from 8 p.m. to 6 a.m. at a time when daylight continued to 10 p.m. That meant that you could not even cross the street to a neighbour's house in the light of day. Suddenly the village was a ghost town, made more so by new regulations on lights and shades. No outside lights were henceforth permitted, and all windows had to be shaded completely so that, at night, absolutely no light was visible from the outside. Failure to shade one's windows adequately implied a desire to help Allied bombers to find their way to Germany, and this was punishable by execution.

If things were tense and sometimes deadly in our village, we heard that they were worse in Amsterdam and other cities. In the summer of 1943, thousands of Amsterdammers walked eastward to the farms of Utrecht, hoping to find food and sleeping wherever they could find refuge. This complicated the Nazis' efforts to control the villages, because the transients were numerous, often unaware of local regulations, and sometimes desperate. From these often unwelcome visitors we learned of the Nazi repression and deportations in the big city. It was surprising that the Nazis allowed these summer migrations to take place, but they seemed to treat them as a safety valve for a city riven by hunger.

But hunger was our problem too, and Arris complained that the visitors took from the farms what she used to be able to bring to us. It was a matter of money too: my father's long-term unemployment was making life financially marginal despite my mother's teaching practice. Student numbers dwindled as fewer villagers could afford the luxury of music lessons in a time of deprivation. But what was the alternative?

Amsterdam's depopulation created an option my father, for the rest of his long life, described as a deal with the devil, a situation that left him no choice. In late 1943 the still-functioning Netherlands Opera in Amsterdam had a dwindling orchestra and needed a concert master. An intermediary asked if he would consider taking the position, in return for a good salary and identity papers that would permit him the *sperrzeit* travel the evening performances would require. There still was a train service between Baarn and Amsterdam, and he would be able to reach the city by bicycle in under two hours, should that be necessary. I did not hear the discussion that led to his decision to accept the assignment, but my mother left me no doubt as to her worries. Being out late at night was dangerous, no matter what permits one might be carrying. And what if the next Nazi authority did not abide by the exemptions of the present one? But my father felt that he had no option under the circumstances. He had to take the risk.

In late 1943, trains were still running and my father would bike to Baarn, catch the Amsterdam train there, and return on the last train from the city. Then came the late-night ride through the forest, past the palace and across the village centre to our house. After several weeks of this he said that he was surprised at the lack of road control by the Nazis: he had been stopped only once although he was out in the open several hours past the *sperrzeit* limit. The town of Baarn and our village looked like ghost towns, he said. Often on his 20-minute ride he did not see a living soul. Moonless nights were especially ghostly: not being allowed to use any light on his bike, he almost literally groped his way back.

But being out, for any reason, entailed huge risks. On the evening of 10 January 1944, Nazi SS officers stopped two members of the underground, who were carrying several German Army uniforms. They escaped in the dark, but not before the identity papers of one of them were checked. The next day, in the neighbourhood revealed by that check, a Nazi patrol stopped three men suspected of being the escapees; one of the Resistance workers took out a pistol and shot an SS officer in the chest. None of this was known to the general public, but on 13 January the Germans retaliated. Driving around in plain clothes, the Nazis took 25 hostages at random from the streets of the village, some before the 8 p.m. curfew and others legally out later. Two of the hostages were killed and left in the street; the others were taken away without notification of their families. My dad was on his way back from Amsterdam, unaware of what was happening. Only luck kept him alive that night.

Incidents like this cast a pall over the village and over the three of us, because we knew that something disastrous could happen at any moment. And yet our daily routine somehow went on; my mother's piano teaching, my rides to school and back, my dad's long trips to and from Amsterdam. One night he was on his way back on the Amsterdam road. Just past the Hilversum intersection, on one of the darkest stretches of the bike path, he thought he heard the word *halt* in the breeze. Uncertain, he stopped – only to find a bayonet, inches from his chest, at a Nazi checkpoint manned by three SS men. He showed his identity papers and was allowed to pass. But had he not heard that soft command, he would not have made it home that evening.

Mr Robert continued to provide news about the war. He had a short-wave radio hidden in a thick book from which the page centres had been cut out, and he could hear the news from London. Reports said that German armies were in retreat from North Africa and Russia, that Sicily had been taken and that Allied troops would soon take Rome. Surely we would be free by the end of 1944! My parents warned me against talking about what I sometimes heard at home, but there were other kids in my third-form class who knew what was happening. We wondered how the kids from NSB families were feeling now. Soon we would be able to raise the Dutch flag again, and display pictures of the Queen, and surely they, the traitors, would be arrested.

My father told me not to get my hopes up. To win the war, he said, the Allies would have to mount an invasion. Unfolding an old *National Geographic* map of Europe, he showed me how far the Allied armies were from us. It proved impossible for the Germans to cross the English Channel to conquer Britain, he said; it would also be very difficult for Allied forces to cross that same Channel to mainland Europe. And even if they did, the German defence would be ferocious. I looked at the map and wondered if the Allies might try to land on the Dutch coast, say between the Maas River and the channel linking Amsterdam to the North Sea. Unlikely, my dad said. Probably somewhere in France. But before that happened, we would have to survive this winter, and the Allies would have to destroy German factories, airfields, bridges and railways. 'The war will come closer to us again,' he warned. 'Remember what to do if you're not home.'

I cannot remember why, but I *was* home in the late morning of 8 March 1944, when all hell broke loose over our village. About 13 kilometres from Soestdijk lay an airfield named Soesterberg, a military airbase. Fighter planes took off from there to confront Allied bombers on their way to Germany, and batteries of anti-aircraft guns encircled it. Soesterberg had been attacked, and was the scene of a heroic defence, during the Nazi invasion of May 1940. We heard stories about that battle, but we were still in the Rotterdam area at the time. Other than the distant rattle of the guns firing at Allied planes overhead and the risk of falling shrapnel, Soesterberg was no factor in our lives. For citizens living on the perimeter of the airfield it was another matter. The Germans confiscated an ever-widening ring of homes around the base, producing a steady stream of refugees.

Shortly after 11 a.m. on 8 March a quiet day suddenly was shattered by the deafening roar of a squadron of low-flying Allied aircraft. I saw some of them out of my window, so close that they seemed to be roiling the tops of the oak trees down our street. My father ordered us downstairs and into the small cellar beneath the kitchen. I grabbed Bobby and climbed down the steep wooden steps. We could hear the familiar sounds of the anti-aircraft guns, but now punctuated by what seemed to be huge explosions. The roar of the planes waxed and waned. 'They're dive-bombing Soesterberg,' said my father. 'Let's hope the people in town are safe.'

The raid went on about a half-hour or so, but my dad would not let us go upstairs until it had been quiet for some time. I was reminded of Rotterdam four years ago, the aeroplane sounds, the bomb shelter. Shortly after noon we got a message from Mr Robert. There had been 20 planes. But what Mr Robert did not know was that the attack was not over. Around 2.30 p.m. an armada of fighter-bombers resumed pounding the airbase with fragmentation bombs. Again we listened in the cellar to the roaring, howling, screaming of the engines, the staccato of the defensive guns, and the thuds of seemingly countless bombs. This attack lasted more than an hour, and the bombers were not very accurate. By nightfall we heard reports of bomb craters even in the pastures of the farms on the edge of our village. Many houses had been hit, and there were civilian casualties. But the airbase had been devastated. The war was back on our doorstep.

The droning of fleets of Allied planes on their way to German targets, and the clatter of cannon firing at them, became part of the daily routine in the spring of 1944. I continued to go to school; my father went back and forth to Amsterdam; and my mother still had a group of piano students. We were undernourished, but we were more fortunate than many others. In the village, as in countless other communities, the Resistance continued to harass the German authorities, risking random retaliation on ordinary citizens.

Occasionally my third-year class met jointly with the fourth-years, whose teacher was Mr Koeman. He was young, energetic and had a great sense of humour, so that classes seemed to pass much more quickly. Mr Koeman was interested in my parents' musical background because his brother was a famous tenor, a career damaged by the war. He was also much more candid about the war and our future than others were. What he said about the Nazis sometimes elicited gasps from my classmates. I wondered what the NSB informers would be saying about him.

Mr Koeman was also a great lunchtime game leader. He devised all manner of competitive games, divided us up into teams and awarded little prizes to the winners. I was good at the geography games, but an also-ran at most of the others. On 6 June

1944 Mr Koeman made an uncharacteristic suggestion: rather than mind games that day, let us go out to the playing field for a ball game.

That is why, on that Tuesday around 1.30 p.m., I was outside in the school grounds when I saw a familiar figure walk up the street towards the fence. It was my father, wearing a long dark raincoat and a scarf. I was astonished to see him in Baarn, outside in the middle of the day, and wondered immediately if he had bad news. I ran over to the fence and my dad stood close on the other side. He looked around and then bent down to tell me what had happened. 'The invasion has begun, son,' he said. 'We may be free by the end of the year. Go back and play. Don't tell anyone.' With a little wave, he walked away. It was cloudy, but no spring day ever looked brighter.

6

HOPE

Racing home on my bike the late afternoon of 6 June 1944, I could hardly contain myself. I wanted to jeer at the Nazis standing guard at the entrance gates of the palace. I wanted to tell the news to a friend going the other way on the bike path. Along the Amsterdam road I saw Mr Robert and waved, and I knew that he knew. I had visions of dinner plates overflowing with food, of Dutch flags snapping in the wind, of late-night walks and bright lights. Oh, how things would soon change!

When I got home, I saw that my father had posted his large *National Geographic* map of Western Europe on the west wall of the second-floor music room. Large red arrows pointed across the English Channel to Normandy in France. A small section of the French coast had already been coloured red. 'They'll probably head for Paris,' my dad said 'If they can hold those beachheads, their weapons and supplies will flow in and then it's just a matter of time. They're all there, you know. The British, the Americans, the Canadians. Probably some Dutch soldiers too, if there were any in England who got away in 1940.'

I looked at the map. It seemed a long way from Normandy to our province, and there were hills and rivers and forests in the way. And after Paris, wouldn't the Allies push into Germany rather than towards us? My father was optimistic. There might be more landings. Allied bombings would clear the way. 'I'm sure you've been taught how to use the scale on a map,' he said. 'Show me how far it is from Paris to Amsterdam.'

I got a piece of paper and laid it along the scale, marked the

56

distance, and measured the imaginary line from Paris to our village. 'About two hundred and sixty,' I said.

'That's miles,' my dad replied. 'The British and the Americans use miles. We use kilometres, remember, so you have to multiply that by one point six. That makes it about four hundred kilometres.'

It seemed to be a huge distance to me. Would the Allies really reach us before the winter?

But in those first weeks after the invasion our spirits soared. It was summer, there was a little more food than there had been during the previous winter and the news from France was good. The red, liberated area on the map grew larger and larger. We heard of the German–Italian retreat in Italy, Nazi setbacks in Russia and Allied victories in the battle for France. High overhead, fleets of Allied bombers droned in huge formations toward their targets in Germany. The anti-aircraft fire from Soesterberg seemed to leave these airborne armadas unaffected.

On Tuesday, 15 August, I was at school when a mass of Allied fighter-bombers (120, as we later found out) roared out of the sky, overflew Baarn and Soestdijk, and attacked the airfield at Soesterberg. Now we had a real reason to perform the safety drill we had practised so often: all classes moved to the hallway in the centre of the main building, where we stood against the walls or sat on the floor. Our school had no basement, so this was the safest place there was; but in the front only the double doors separated us from the outside. So we could hear the bombardment and sometimes were able to see several planes making their turns for the attack. Mr Koeman watched the assault from a classroom window upstairs, and came down to tell us what was happening. My father, who was home, told me that he had seen only one Allied plane shot down. The next day we began to hear news of the damage: the bombing had not been very accurate. More bomb craters pocked the farms on Soestdijk's outskirts. But some runways remained usable. 'They'll have to come back,' my father said.

About a week later something strange happened at school. Mr Koeman was teaching us a history lesson when we heard loud voices outside the classroom. One of those voices unmistakably was that of the headmaster, but this time he was not berating an offending student. He was arguing with adults, and the argument was punctuated by what sounded like boots marching up the stairs and across the hall to his office. A door slammed, and the dispute continued; our classroom was adjacent to Mr van Dijk's office, and obviously there was trouble.

A few moments later our classroom door swung open, and in marched two uniformed German officers, followed by Mr van Dijk. The Germans looked around the room, and one walked to the window to look at the grounds; Mr van Dijk and Mr Koeman exchanged an anguished glance. Mr van Dijk's face was beet-red, even more so than it usually was after one of his outbursts. Presently the Germans nodded and left, crossing the hall to the sixth-year classroom. Mr Koeman covered his eyes and shook his head, but held up his other hand to keep us from talking. He told us to keep quiet and to read our textbook. With that, he slipped out of the door.

What was happening was that the Nieuwe Baarnse School had become a target of Nazi confiscation practices, although that did not occur to me, nor, I think, to any of us in the class that day. The German officers were there to inspect and assess the space and facilities, and as it turned out we were fortunate: they would give Mr van Dijk and his staff several days to prepare for the evacuation. More often families were ousted summarily and allowed to take only what they could carry out of their homes in a few hours. Mr van Dijk and his teachers wisely told none of us what lay ahead. The next day, school continued as though nothing had happened.

But the principal and his staff did notify as many parents as they could reach that the school would be taken over and that alternative space was being sought. Parents were asked not to discuss this with their children, and mine said nothing to me; but of course the rumour did spread in Baarn. Nothing at school suggested that any dislocation lay in store, however, and I paid no attention.

But the war itself *was* becoming a factor in daily life. On Sunday afternoon, 3 September 1944, I was playing with Bernard and Paul in the Batenburgs' back garden when suddenly another wave of Allied planes approached, and an attack on Soesterberg began again. We ran indoors and, until my father ordered us into the cellar, saw that this was a different encounter: the anti-aircraft capabilities of Soesterberg had obviously been improved since the attack three weeks earlier. The response from the ground was thunderous, and we could hear the clatter of shrapnel and the breaking of windows; smoky trails rose towards the bombers and the staccato of gunfire became a continuous roar. The aircraft engines sounded like thunder, shaking the house as they aimed at the airfield at rooftop height. It was by far the most intensive bombing yet, involving as many as 150 planes that kept up a two-hour barrage; now, finally, the airfield was being destroyed. The anti-aircraft guns were nearly silenced, finally responding only in occasional bursts. A pall of smoke rose above Soesterberg and drifted towards us. Homes were on fire in neighbouring Soest as well as on the airport perimeter, and again there were civilian casualties. We hoped that this would be the end of the airfield as a strategic base, and as a target.

One of my classmates, Eppo Jansen, lived up the street from us, near where the paved road ended at a large open space we called the Eng. Eppo's house overlooked the Eng, and apparently one of the Allied bombers had mistaken this field for the airbase. At school the next day he told us what happened: the attacker had come from behind their house and flown directly over the Eng, dropping a half dozen bombs as he went. The Jansens had no cellar, so Eppo was in the front hall and, through the small front-door window, saw the bombs explode and the earth blow up in what he described as a fountain of soil. Fortunately the angle of the bombs was away from his house, which shook but came through it all unscathed.

Then, suddenly, my years at the Nieuwe Baarnse School ended. A few days after the latest Soesterberg attack the teachers issued us all with a note that announced the imminent confiscation of the premises and the news that an alternative building had been found. As much of the school's contents as could be accommodated there would be moved to the new locale over the weekend, and classes would resume the following Monday. Since the new location would be a large but still inadequate private home, classes would have to be combined and the standards of the school might be somewhat affected.

The new address turned out to be on the very road I normally rode along, the main street to Baarn after the Hilversum turn-off, and therefore closer to home than the school itself was. It was a large, beautiful but neglected villa with spacious rooms, two sunrooms with huge windows framed by ivy, and three upstairs bedrooms. The headmaster, teachers, staff and some townspeople had loaded desks, tables, bookcases and other furniture on carts and wagons and had managed to get the 'school' ready for us after the weekend. I liked the setting right across from the forest; and we fourth-years had a bright, airy room with large windows and billowing, sheer curtains that softened the light. Mr van Dijk visited every class on the first morning, asking us to cooperate by being disciplined and hard-working, and not to complain.

We soon knew why he had done so. Wartime logistics made things tough on the teachers; supplies ran out, including ink and chalk; and in any case, the portable blackboards were too few and had to be moved from room to room. It was getting colder, but to conserve what little fuel there was, the heat was not turned on. But I felt safer. Not only was this building much closer to home (I could walk it at a fast clip in 40 minutes, I soon learned), but it also had a basement. On our first day we practised the emergency drill that led down the cellar stairs to an area that could accommodate us all. You could even sit on one of several rolls of carpet the owners of the villa had left there.

In the classrooms we continued our lessons in history, arithmetic, the Dutch language and other basic subjects. I especially liked the language classes, taught by Mr van Dijk, who now seemed far less fearsome than he had been before we moved. Every day there was a spelling exercise: Mr van Dijk would say 20 difficult words, and we would have to spell them. He then corrected all the lists and returned them. One day I had them all correct and he wrote *hulde* (homage) on my paper. That moved me – I thought such a word applied only to royalty.

In truth, learning was a bit chaotic in the new setting. But I enjoyed the atmosphere. It was almost like being home: there was a sense that we were all in this together, and that we would make the best of it. On some days the sounds of war intruded, and during the emergency drill we were reminded of the dangers, present and future. On the busy street outside, columns of military vehicles ranging from armoured cars to tanks moved past. Sometimes we would hear and feel the cadence of marching brigades as German troops proceeded from the railway station nearby to their defensive positions.

And homework continued. This created new problems: as autumn daylight shortened and the electricity supply faltered, it was better to get this done before dark. But the tyres on my bike had worn out and were beyond repair, so that I was walking back and forth to school, getting home not much before 5 p.m. on a good day.

Meanwhile, the red areas on my father's map grew ever larger. Paris had fallen to the Allies, Belgium was being liberated. In our village, the Nazis were confiscating every vehicle: not just men's and women's bicycles, but also carts and wagons. Members of the Resistance as well as the general public sabotaged the Germans by throwing nails and broken glass on the bike paths and roadways; since all vehicles now belonged to the Nazis, all damage inflicted would be on the occupiers. The German authorities issued an order that stated that all houses in the village would be burned down if this activity did not stop. The sabotage continued. A response would have to come.

Without transportation, and with the railway system disrupted by Allied bombing, my father had no way to reach Amsterdam, where despite hunger and despair the opera had continued to function. This was the end of his work there, but not before he had some dreadful experiences. Things were much worse in the city than in our village; as early as the autumn of 1944 people were dying of hunger there. One member of my father's orchestra succumbed to starvation during the evening of a performance. That same day he had seen a wagonload of corpses being taken to the morgue. He was shaken by what he had seen and frightened by the proximity of such horror to our village. How long would it be before we faced the same fate?

To such dark thoughts, I found the ever-redder map on the wall of the music room a wonderful antidote. Maps can be used to convey propaganda, to depict danger, to stake claims – but this map imparted hope. Whenever my spirits sank I would look at some of the towns in the liberated area and visualize what life would be like there. They, too, had waited for the Allied advance to reach them, and surely they also had their moments of despair. But the map seemed to prove the inevitability of the coming German defeat. I would colour our province red the day the Allies marched up the Amsterdam road.

But on 17 September our spirits soared. At mid-morning, the sky suddenly was filled by wave after wave of Allied planes, all headed in a generally easterly direction. They were flying fairly low, unlike the bombers heading for Germany. Fighter planes flying above as well as below the armada provided protection, although there was hardly any response from Soesterberg. This, we knew, was no mission to Germany. Nor was it another attack on Soesterberg. These planes were spearheading a landing somewhere, and surely this signaled the beginning of the war's end.

My mother worked off her excitement by playing her Hanon exercises on the music-room piano; she played with such force that she sounded like a machine-gun. My father ran up and down the stairs, trying to get a better view of the planes. Presently, even before the last planes had passed overhead, our doorbell rang. Mr Robert's son, a boy my age, delivered a note addressed to my father. It said that parachutists were landing near a town named Arnhem, not far from us at all. An Allied bridgehead would be established on the Rhine, enabling the liberating forces to cross. Soon the heartland of the Netherlands would be free.

It was a beautiful autumn day, the sun shining brightly and just a few clouds in the sky. The fleet of aircraft overhead seemed almost serene, flying in unbroken formation and without the thunderous extremes of the attacks on Soesterberg. Even the fighter planes flew in lazy circles. Had the Germans decided not to challenge this force at all? My father peered at the map, on which the first red areas to touch the Netherlands – in the south-eastern province of Limburg had already been shaded. 'Just imagine,' my dad said. 'In Maastricht today you can hang out the Dutch flag, eat adequately, live without fear of Nazi retaliation. Soon the Arnhemmers will experience this too, thanks to those heroes in the planes up there.' With that he took his pencil and coloured Arnhem and environs red.

I looked at the map and remembered my doubts in June. But the nearest red areas still seemed far away from us; and while Arnhem was close, it was quite distant from the liberated parts of our country. And all of Germany to the east of us still was in Nazi hands – under constant bombing, yes, but not yet in Allied hands. Looking at my dad's red mark around Arnhem, it seemed to be just a small island in a still vast German domain.

The four of us stayed in the music room, my mother now playing Beethoven's 'Appassionata' (the association has been lifelong for me), my father looking at the atlas of the Netherlands, which had a detailed map of the Arnhem area, Bobby sleeping through it all on the couch. We wondered how many planes had already passed and were still coming; it must be in the hundreds. Occasionally we heard the muffled sound of an explosion in the far distance. 'The first of them should be on the ground now,' said my father. 'The first night will be critical.'

The following day brought exciting confirmation: Allied forces had parachuted into the Arnhem area and were meeting stiff, but not insurmountable resistance. Soon both sides of the river would have Allied bridgeheads, and then the way would be cleared for massive forces to cross the Rhine. We would see additional paratroops being flown into the Arnhem area. We might be free by Christmas after all, possibly even by Santa Claus Day.

But towards the evening of that second day my father got the first hint that things were not going so well at Arnhem. German resistance was more powerful than expected. There were supply problems. A further paratroop landing was impractical. Something was going wrong with the Allied strategy. Briefly there was hope of a reversal of fortunes, but as the days wore on the awful truth came out: the Battle of Arnhem was lost. On 25 September my father erased his red mark on Arnhem. Nor were there other areas to shade. The Allied advance seemed to have stalled, and we faced the dreadful prospect of another winter under Nazi rule.

The Allied defeat at Arnhem seemed to have a direct impact on our village. The Nazi authorities revelled in the people's disappointment and hardened their measures of control. Following their victory, they forcibly evacuated virtually the entire population of Arnhem, scattering it into the countryside all around. Hundreds of refugees arrived in Soestdijk, already overburdened with immigrants from other directions, notably Amsterdam. About the same time, Mr Batenburg got advance warning of a massive *razzia* to be staged in October: all men between the ages of 17 and 50 still in the village would have to present themselves to an army post; if still in possession of any kind of vehicle, that should be brought along, as well as a shovel, a plate and a spoon.

Mr Batenburg urged my father to leave the village before this order became official. My father learned that the train from Baarn to Groningen in the northern part of the Netherlands, where his parents lived, was still running although irregularly. He decided to leave immediately, and in a matter of hours we were on our way along the Amsterdam Road towards the station. Our neighbour Mr Richter offered to help, going some distance ahead of us and thus alerting us to any checkpoints on the way to Baarn. He, a man in his seventies, would create a scene at any checkpoint, diverting attention and allowing my parents time to get away. But as it happened, we reached Baarn without incident, and were not accosted as we waited for the train to Groningen. Late that afternoon we reached the home of my father's parents and moved in.

My parents were unsure of the length of our visit, but a visit it would have to be; Groningen was a city, and the food situation there was precarious. Still, we stayed for several weeks, long enough for me to be put in a school and to discover the differences between Holland Dutch and Groningen Dutch. My spelling tests in Groningen accrued a failing grade. *Scheepstimmerwerven,* the teacher thought she said. *Skeepstimmerwerben,* I heard her say.

I remember that it was never clear to me why we went to Groningen at such short notice, taking Bobby with us, nor was I told why we went back when we did. I was told about Mr Batenburg's warning only later. But when we got back home, I walked up to the music room to look at the map. Groningen lay even farther from the advancing Allied forces than Soestdijk, so it must be better to be closer. On the other hand, life in Groningen seemed to be less tense than in our village; there were fewer Nazi patrols in evidence and I never once had to go indoors because of an air raid. But my grandparents also suffered from food shortages, and my grandfather, who worked for the Netherlands Railways and thus had access to extra supplies now and then, said that things were getting worse in the city. So when my father got word via the Resistance that the round-up of men in the Soestdijk area had taken place and was over, he decided to return to the village. We went in the nick of time: a few days later the entire country's electrical system was disrupted, and long-distance train transport came to an end.

In Groningen I had forgotten how much solace a map could provide. Back home I stared at it for a long time, hoping that, in the weeks of our absence, some areas would have fallen to the Allies and would be coloured in. I noticed that my dad had failed to erase all the red from the Arnhem area. Maybe Mr Robert would have some good news. But looking out of the window I could see that winter was closing in on us. It was now the fourth week of October, and the fall had come early. It was cold and damp and bleak, and darkness came early. And I wondered how my walks to and from school would feel in the gloomy forest.

My father that evening reported that there was something that passed for good news. The Nazis who had for some time run the local administration (and who had mobilised that round-up of able-bodied men) had been reassigned elsewhere, and a new regime had settled into Nazi headquarters along the Amsterdam road. It might be some time before these new commanders became familiar with the village, and who knew, perhaps this would be a milder Nazi team.

Such were the remnants of hope in Soestdijk in the late autumn of 1944.

7

TERROR

War and military occupation give rise to the most amazing social contradictions. Some aspects of daily routine continue: family meals even if food is in short supply, religious ritual even if reduced to small private gatherings, schooling for youngsters even under makeshift circumstances. Citizens cooperate and help each other, but they must also compete for survival. Luxury items such as cigarettes become more valuable than money, and can buy what money cannot. Some families, having had the foresight to hoard such items, now trade them for food, and jealous townspeople call them OW-ers, people who are beneficiaries of war. Others, the NSB families, live comparatively well because they receive rewards from the occupiers for spying and betraying their neighbours. Ordinary citizens are at constant risk of arrest and disappearance, execution, military action, mistaken identity or unwitting contravention of some regulation.

I have much to be grateful for to my parents, but nothing exceeds my appreciation for their efforts to make my wartime childhood as normal as possible under such conditions. They were determined that I should go to school as long as it was possible. They allowed me to play across the street when other children were being kept inside. They managed for a very long time to keep me unaware of the worst of the dangers we faced. They instilled in me a confidence that whatever was happening to others, we would be all right.

My mother told me years later that watching me walk away in the morning to school in Baarn was her most difficult moment;

66

and often she and Bobby stood in the street to watch for me walking back along the Amsterdam road. Bobby, having decided that if adults spent their day walking upright she should do so too, would stand on her hind legs, leaning against my mother and wagging her tail when she recognized me. When I walked along the south side of the street, I would first see the graceful Viersprong, the inn that dominated the village centre, and then my mother and Bobby would come into view. The Viersprong in the warm season had colourful, striped umbrellas on its patio, and even during the 1944 summer, when the restaurant had long since closed, these were opened to brighten up the scene. By late October, the umbrellas were folded up but the lights would be on, a pretty picture and a beacon as I came home.

That tranquil scene was one of those wartime contradictions. For all the misery Soestdijk was experiencing, the village centre remained as pleasant-looking as it always was. Across from the Viersprong, behind a low stone wall, stood the tree-shaded buildings of Marienburg, a Roman Catholic convent that occupied the whole inside corner of the bend in the Amsterdam road. It was flanked by ponds crossed by ornate wooden bridges and wide, leaf-strewn walkways; on special occasions there would be colourful, elaborate processions along these paths and across the bridges. These festivities had continued until well into 1944. On the other side of the convent stood the centre's dominant structure, a large seventeenth-century church with a tall steeple. Services there continued until the Nazis issued an order banning gatherings of more than four unrelated people. And on the opposite side was a small row of local shops that, in better times, sold baked goods, flowers and groceries. Now there were some signs of neglect, but the grace of the Viersprong and the tall oak trees, the architecture of the convent and the tower of the church made for a reassuring continuity.

Headmaster van Dijk obviously shared my parents' views regarding the importance of daily routine. Our school hours remained the same as they had always been, and I went to school six days a week, with half days on Wednesdays and Saturdays. And homework was not any less than it had been before. But now electricity supply to the village was intermittent, and getting that homework done before dark was not easy as the days of autumn shortened. Still, it kept my mind off other things. There was little time for playing (or, fortunately, for violin practice). Wednesdays, Saturdays and Sundays were the best days. And I considered myself lucky in that my parents were not religious. Bernard and Paul complained that much of their Sunday was taken up by Sunday school, Bible classes and religious services.

That is why on Wednesday, 25 October 1944, I was at home in the early afternoon, reading a book in my room, when we came close to disaster. Arris, our maid, who also worked for other families in the neighbourhood, usually was next door at the Ladies Bakker's, but I saw her running up the pavement through our gate to the front door. She frantically rang our doorbell and pounded on it at the same time. 'Open up!' she shouted. 'Get this door open!'

I heard my mother rushing to the door. Before she could ask what the matter was, Arris shouted that the Viersprong was 'going'.

'What do you mean, the Viersprong is going?' my mother asked.

'Don't ask questions now!' cried Arris. "The Resistance did something yesterday and now the Nazis are blowing up the Viersprong! We've got twenty minutes to help people move out! They're putting in the dynamite now! Come on!' And with this, she ran down the street to the inn. From the front window, I could see other people rushing toward the Viersprong, and a large green truck was parked near the little park. German soldiers were running cables from the truck to the Viersprong.

My father suddenly was nowhere to be seen. Having told me to stay inside my mother followed Arris, and looking down the street I could see Germans in uniform with machine-guns pointed towards the inn. Traffic barricades were being set up on all streets leading to the village centre. Across the street I could see Bernard and Paul at the window of the Batenburgs' house.

After a few minutes my mother came back with two armloads of belongings, including a painting she dragged along by its hanging wire. Arris, sweating profusely and breathing heavily, threw down another load. They ran off again, and came back with some other things. Then, just as they were about to run down again, a deafening explosion shook the neighbourhood, breaking every window facing the Viersprong. People rushed indoors in all directions as a second blast sent the Viersprong's huge roof flying everywhere. Soon the beautiful old building was engulfed in flames so high that I could see them over the Ladies Bakker's house. I wondered what would become of the house of Dr Kok, the vet who lived next to the Viersprong and whose son was one of my friends. Leaning out of our rear first-floor bathroom, I could see the shimmering, brocaded curtains of the inn's second floor as they were consumed by fire. Inside, works of art melted in the flames. The inferno grew as pieces of burning tinder flew in all directions. An acrid smoke enveloped the neighbourhood. Shards of glass littered the streets. The people whose home this had been stood weeping across from the burning building. Now the commander of the operation ordered everyone inside or away from the scene.

Hours later, when the fire had died down and a pile of smouldering rubble was all that remained of the Viersprong, I walked down the block. All the windows of Dr Kok's house had been blown out. His son, who was my age, just stood and stared; he did not answer me when I spoke to him. Looking westward from his house, with the Viersprong gone, you could now see all the way down the road toward Amsterdam. The trees near the inn had been incinerated. The heart of the village had been ripped out.

My father had been prudent to hide. Even as Arris and my mother were sorting and stacking the salvaged goods that lay in our hallway, Nazi soldiers came to the door demanding to see any men in the house. Perhaps it was my mother's withering look, possibly Bobby's endless barking, but they left without doing a search. Still, I did not see him until the following morning.

My parents kept me home that next day, and around midday Mr Batenburg came over to talk about what had happened. He had been a visitor to the Viersprong all his life. In better days people had promenaded along the curving pavement in front of the inn and had taken tea on the terrace outside the elegant dining room with its Delft-tiled fireplace. Prominent guests had stayed at the

69

Viersprong for generations, and the visitor's book, undoubtedly burned, had in it the names of many famous and well-connected people, even royalty. Long-term residents had lived on the upper floor under the sweep of the red-tiled roof. All this was rubble now. Mr Batenburg wiped away a tear.

And the Nazis were not finished. Even as Mr Batenburg sat in our living room, they destroyed without warning and without any evacuation time our area's most prominent and architecturally historic farm, the Kok Estate (no relation to our vet neighbour). Buildings, barns and stables were dynamited and consumed by fire in little more than an hour. By late afternoon my father had learned the reason for the Nazis' retaliation: the Resistance had cut several power lines leading to the German headquarters on the Amsterdam road.

On Friday morning my parents decided to send me back to school, and as I walked down the street in the early morning I saw one of the most depressing sights of the war. Dozens of people, perhaps as many as a hundred, were digging in the ruins of the Viersprong, some of them with their bare hands. They were pulling out pieces of twisted metal, remnants of partially burned wood, broken tiles, even bricks. It reminded me of an ant heap. I supposed that some of those people were residents who had been forced to leave almost everything they owned behind, but others must be scavengers, even souvenir hunters. Maybe the NSB family up Mecklenburglaan (formerly Wilhelminalaan) would like a memento, I thought grimly.

In truth the Nazi retaliation on Soestdijk had been relatively mild. News spread through the village of the dreadful fate of the village of Putten, not that far away, where all 400 citizens – men, women, children had been murdered by the Nazis in reprisal for acts of sabotage. My mother recalled that the Nazis had threatened to burn down every house in Soestdijk if the Resistance continued its activities. Were a few successes that did little more than inconvenience the Germans worth the risk to every life and all property in our community? I wondered what kids my age would have thought, there in Putten, when the Nazis with their machine-guns

70

lined them up with their parents against the barn walls and started shooting. For the first time I could remember, fear began to invade my night's sleep. I dreamed of round-ups and fires and killings, and awoke from nightmares.

The Nazi regime now began to tighten the restrictions on daily life, and to make ordinary citizens responsible for vigilance against sabotage. We already lived under *sperrzeit* regulations, which limited the hours we were allowed out on the street. Now the Nazis proclaimed a *sperrgebiet* policy which designated certain areas in our village and environs as restricted at virtually all times. Such areas were delimited because of their supposed strategic nature, or because they were associated in some way with Resistance activities. If one's house happened to lie in such a designated *sperrgebiet*, one was allowed outside for only one hour, from 5.00 p.m. to 6.00 p.m. daily. Posted orders on noticeboards, trees and walls included maps showing the locations of *sperrgebiete*. Citizens disobeying the rules would be shot on sight. People unaware of the existence of a *sperrgebiet*, and who walked through it on the way to work, school or home, would not be spared.

In addition, the Nazis assigned the security of some portion of a railway line, bridge, dike or other facility to a village neighbourhood. Villagers were ordered to stand watch around the clock: old men, women, even children. Should something happen to what was deemed to be a strategic structure, those on whose watch this occurred would be held responsible and executed. We knew it was no idle threat. We remembered Putten.

The first three blocks along our street got such an assignment in late November, and my father was unsure whether to hide or to participate. His fear was that my mother would be conscripted, leaving me alone in case something happened. He was still in possession of his special permit from his opera period, so he might escape arrest on the way. From the Resistance, via Mr Robert, he had assurance that no act of sabotage was planned. So he spent a week's nights walking along a stretch of the railway line from Soestdijk to Baarn while my mother worried.

Others were not so fortunate. Those on watch risked not only Nazi retaliation, but also Allied attack on the facility they were

71

guarding. When Allied planes attacked a bridge not far from Baarn, one villager was killed and several wounded. It fell to my father and a colleague to go to the man's house and inform his wife of what had happened. He came home terribly upset and my mother wept as he told her the story.

Across the street at the Batenburgs, another drama was unfolding. Their oldest son, Noud, lay dying of polio. More than a year earlier, he had fallen ill while working in a conscripted labour gang. My mother saw him come home in his green uniform, struggling to reach their front door. At first it seemed that he was just weak from a severe flu, but soon it became clear that Noud was stricken with something much more serious. Noud was in his mid-twenties, a handsome and friendly man with a cheerful disposition. When he became permanently bedridden the Batenburgs placed him in a downstairs room large enough to hold as many as a dozen visitors. When I was over playing with Paul and Bernard, we would always take time to visit him. At night, when we defied the curfew and dashed across the street for a visit, we would all gather in Noud's room.

In the spring of 1944 Noud already was paralysed from the waist down, and weakness was affecting his left arm. But he always talked optimistically about life after the war. Resting against the pillows he still looked good, well-groomed. In October, when my family had fled to Groningen in advance of the Nazi search for men, the Germans came to the Batenburgs' home and found Noud in his room. They assumed that he was pretending to be ill, and dragged him from his bed. He fell in a heap on the floor; the Nazis kicked him and poked him with rifle butts. Apparently persuaded that he really was ill and incapacitated, they marched out of the house, slamming the door without a word. But Noud's positive attitude never wavered. He never complained about the pain and indignity that had been visited upon him; his faith sustained him. With his small hand mirror he could see out of the side window of his room, and watch the Allied bomber fleets pass overhead. 'I'd rather be here than up there,' he said after we watched a B-21, hit by anti-aircraft fire, disintegrate in a ball of flame.

From the German command post, one edict followed another.

We were reminded that a total blackout prevailed, and to make the point some German police rode about town and shot into homes where the flicker of a candle or dynamo light could be seen. Gatherings of more than four persons not part of an immediate family were forbidden, making our occasional forays to the Batenburgs even more dangerous. One morning we found posted on the large oak tree near our house an order that every house with a front garden had to have a hole dug in it, no less than 1 metre 20 centimetres deep and over 80 centimetres wide, and, if the yard was wide enough, about 5.5 metres apart. Inspection of the readied foxholes (for that was what was intended) would occur on 3 December. People who did not have such a hole ready would be subject to arrest. We wondered how the Ladies Bakker and old man Richter could be compelled to do what was ordered. My father assumed that the turnover of authority would obviate the inspection. It did. We worried, but we never heard about this edict again.

Meanwhile, the circumstances of life deteriorated to unimaginable levels. We all became scavengers, thieves. Food was in desperately short supply. My father had obtained the carcass of a pig, which hung in the frigid attic upstairs. Salted and dried, this provided us with some fat; each day he would cut off three small pieces of it for lunch. It smelled and tasted terrible, but it was food, and with the fruit and nuts from the garden, stored in the basement, we felt fortunate indeed. My dad also had built a hen house and pen in the back of the garden, and by December 1944 we had one egg-laying hen left. Her eggs were, literally, life-savers.

Along with food, firewood was a key to survival. The nearby Crown Domain forests had been fenced off by the Germans, but there were still trees in gardens, parks and vacant sites. I found a stand of large holly tree in a corner of the grounds of a large, abandoned estate on the road to Amsterdam. Every day for more than a week I would climb over the wall and cut down a tree, hack off the branches, tie a rope around the trunk and drag it home. My parents cheered this effort, and our hoard of firewood grew daily. But one afternoon, struggling with an especially large tree, I was late getting away – and was caught by two watchmen checking on the property. They grabbed me and threw me to the ground, took my axe from me, and rode off on their bikes. I ran after them scream-ing, realizing that the loss of an axe at a time like this could spell disaster. I have been lucky many times in my life, and this was one such time. The men had been asked to stop by the house of Mr Richter, ironically to cut down some of his remaining trees. I ran into our house and told my dad what had happened. He went next door and came back with the axe. But I was shaken and gave up the search for wood for the time being.

Still, we did need more firewood. As December grew colder and darker it was clear that our supply would not last the winter. One day before Christmas my father was told that firewood was for sale at a farm about 8 kilometres away. He borrowed a hand-cart with two large, wooden-spoked wheels and the three of us, dressed in our warmest clothes, started the long walk.

To get this far, you went along the road towards Utrecht about 2 kilometres, and then there was a dirt path into the woods. It was (of course, this being Holland) raining, and the forest floor as well as the path were matted with wet, shiny leaves. Presently we reached something I had not seen before: a toll barrier. A rough wooden beam stretched across the path, with a post and wooden peg at one end and a V-shaped catch at the other. A heavy stone hung from the piece that extended beyond the post. In a small cubicle sat a man in blue overalls. It cost 10 cents for him to lift the barrier. I wondered how many people would come by here in a day, for it to be worth his sitting there. Of course we would not be the only ones looking for wood, but that forest path seemed pretty lonely.

At the farmhouse, logs were arranged in stacks, and I realized how futile my forays to the holly trees had been. What riches lay here: thick trunks, thinner ones, kindling. My dad negotiated with the owner and we loaded our cart. Since the house sat on a slight hill, the three of us had no trouble pushing it towards the toll path, and then some distance towards the main road. But then the ground levelled out, and we had more than we could handle. Beneath the leaves, the path had ruts, and these turned muddy. About halfway to the main road, the wheels of our loaded cart sank into the mud and we could not budge it again.

I could see us abandoning our hoard right there, but my dad had an idea. He told my mother and me to wait, walked back to the farm, and in half an hour came back with a farm boy and a horse. The boy tied the horse's harness to the cart, gave him a pat on the flank, and the cart moved as though it weighed nothing. When we approached the toll booth, the boy ordered the guard to lift the beam so we would not have to stop, even before my dad paid another 10 cents. By mid-afternoon we were at the paved road; the boy untied the horse, took his tip, lifted his cap and left, and we resumed pushing towards home.

The Utrecht road passed along the side of the palace grounds, and then you would turn right onto the road from Amsterdam. Here the land lay virtually flat, and once we had some momentum we could keep the loaded wagon moving pretty well. We passed Mr Robert's house, and approached the ruins of the Viersprong. But now we faced another problem: the street was hard enough, but past the remnants of the Viersprong it sloped slightly upward. That was enough to stop us dead in our tracks. We were also running out of steam; it was late afternoon, getting dark, and we had not eaten anything since a meagre breakfast very early in the morning. Soon the curfew would start, and if we had to abandon our treasure here on a street corner, it would surely be gone in the morning.

My father had another idea. He got a large stone, and put it under one wheel. We grabbed the spokes of the other wheel, moved it as far as we could, and then put the stone under that wheel. We inched forward, but we would not make it by dark. So we reverted to my holly-tree technique: we rolled the logs onto the ground, tied a rope around each, and dragged them the last 200 metres home. Just as it got dark, the cart had become light enough so that we could push the rest of the cargo uphill and into our garden.

Over the next week I had the job of sawing the logs into stove-sized pieces and splitting these in four. This way the stash looked even bigger, and I lined all of it up against a wall inside the shed. I found that such hard work was one way to still my hunger. For some reason I was less hungry after a day's fairly hard labour than when I sat around the house.

For all of us, hunger was becoming as constant a companion as danger. My parents had some connections – a farmer who would give us some milk now and then, a friend who got us some grain. The authorities had organized a soup kitchen where you could trade coupons for a watery stew, and I went twice a week with a pan to get our share. Somehow my mother always managed to convert it into something more substantial. Our garden not only produced fruit, but also potatoes and some vegetables. But by late December our basement supply was beginning to run out. We heard ominous news of villagers dying of starvation, or of complications brought on by malnutrition. My dad's weight seemed to be dropping daily. My mother's wiry build concealed her condition, but her face showed it. I was hollow-cheeked, skin and bones.

But on a good day, there would be bread to share, and my mother would find a way to make tea from endlessly reused tea leaves. Thinnest of us all was Bobby the dog. We had always walked her on a leash, but now there were good reasons to let her go out: no one should be in the street unless it was absolutely necessary, and she might find herself something to eat. One unforgettable day she came home with something large in her mouth, and laid it down on the kitchen floor at my mother's feet. It was an egg, and not one from our own garden. How far she might have roamed to find it was anyone's guess; how she brought it home without breaking it was a miracle. I still feel guilty about what happened next: my mother boiled it and we divided it in four , but Bobby got very little of it.

The red areas on the map in the music room now seemed to expand more slowly, at least in our direction. The Allied campaign eastward was in full swing, but we realized that liberation would not come until the winter of 1945, or later. We were frequently reminded of the dangers we faced. A stray bomb fell on a house a couple of blocks away, killing an entire family; when we walked over to view the scene we noted that the upper floor, which had collapsed into the ground floor, had less damage than those below. The bomb had apparently exploded in the basement or on the ground floor. In any case, my father decided that we would start sleeping in the same room, in a safer part of the house. We also started sleeping in our clothes, with a packed suitcase for each of us at the ready. In case of a night-time *razzia*, we would all go, and try to stay together as long as we could.

Sleeping in the same room had another advantage: it provided some warmth during the long, cold nights. We tried to use our firewood sparingly, starting a fire in the early evening, but by midnight a bone-chilling cold overtook the house. My dad had wrapped old clothes, blankets, paper and rags around every water pipe to which he had access, and we left taps dripping. In the morning, there often would be a film of ice on the water in the toilet. You were so stiff with cold that getting up seemed to risk cracking a joint, or breaking a bone.

Santa Claus Day had passed, and so had Christmas. By now we occupied only the kitchen at the back of the house and the bedroom upstairs; the rest of the house was closed up, except for Sundays. Only when the sun shone and the temperature rose would we open other rooms. We waited for a repeat of Arnhem, except with a better result: a fleet of planes, parachutists dropping, the end of misery. When we said goodnight in the evening of 31 December, we knew that the New Year would be the year of liberation. If we survived.

The morning of 1 January 1945 was clear, bright and, as usual, freezing. I was still in bed, wearing socks and gloves, my head under the blankets, when I heard the sound of approaching planes. That was nothing unusual; the drone of the bombers on their way to Germany was an almost daily (mostly nightly) accompaniment to life. But this, I soon realized, was unusual. The sound got louder and louder, and it was coming from an unfamiliar direction. Usually, the action came from the west or southwest, including the attacks on Soesterberg and the armada aimed at Arnhem. But these planes were coming from the north and north-east. They were flying low, but there was none of the noise associated with dive-bombing.

The sound grew into a sustained roar. I got up and ran to the back of the house, where the bathroom window looked in the direction of Amersfoort. What I saw made me gasp. Warplanes by

77

the hundreds, flying at low altitude, literally darkened the sky. There were large, slow ones and small, faster ones; single-engined, twin-engined, large four-engined bombers. All of them were heading south, and I could clearly see their markings, even the crews in some of the cockpits. These were German warplanes, and they were heading for Allied lines.

For some time the Nazis had been promising a counter-offensive that would push the Allies back to the English Channel, but it had been so unlikely that no one took it seriously. What did the retreating Germans have left? How could they inflict any consequential damage on the advancing Allies? But as the seemingly endless fleet of planes passed overhead, our hearts sank. The Germans would not drive the Allies back, but this might further delay their progress towards us.

What we witnessed, I learned much later, was Operation Bodenplatte, the code name for the German surprise attack to open the New Year. It was a coordinated air and ground attack timed to strike when the Allied forces were supposed to be in a post-New Year's Eve state of low alert. It did substantial damage, and it undoubtedly delayed our liberation. The Resistance reported that part of Operation Bodenplatte had been aimed at Allied forces in northern Belgium and the southern Netherlands, and that roads and bridges leading towards us had been destroyed. It was not a good way to start the New Year.

Wartime creates intellectual and cultural as well as material deprivations. Without radios (and in any case without electricity), without concerts or movies or other diversion, some people would do almost anything for cultural stimulation (just as others would trade food for cigarettes). My parents traded books with neighbours and friends, some of them so broken and dog-eared that the pages had to be kept together by twine.

During the winter of 1945 my parents began offering a series of weekly 'house concerts' in our living room on Sunday afternoons. These concerts violated the ban on gatherings of more than four unrelated people, but all comers were familiar with the circumstances. They would start arriving singly or as couples, some as long as an hour before the 2.30 p.m. starting time. Most would walk around the side of the house to the kitchen door at the back. The front door was left unlocked for people to enter quickly. From the street you could not see into the living room because the raised piano lid blocked the view.

I had the job of setting up the living and dining rooms with all available chairs, a total of nearly 40. It was cold, but over three dozen people warmed the place up considerably, and my father lit a wood fire in the stove. After the concert started Arris would boil water over the coal fire in the kitchen. One of the concertgoers had contributed some coal, and another a tin of precious tea. She had tea ready when intermission came. Afterwards, people left in small numbers via both doors at suitable intervals.

These house concerts were one way my parents could earn some of the means of survival. The price of admission was a piece of firewood or any kind of food (a potato, an egg, an apple). These would accumulate by the front and back doors and I would put them away. One day someone brought an unbelievable gift: a small loaf of bread. It lay on the small stack of firewood others had brought, and I excitedly told my mother about it. I put it on the kitchen counter – but when, that Sunday, the audience had left, the loaf was gone. My mother said that she understood how this could happen. 'Don't blame whoever it was,' she said. 'She may have a son your age in her house. I might steal it myself under the same circumstances.'

For me those house concerts made for wonderful weekends in a dismal winter. I heard much of the repertoire into which I had, literally, been born, and the music brought happy memories. For one day, the house was comparatively warm, and our confinement was broken. After the intermission, when Arris and I washed and dried the cups and saucers, I kept the kitchen door open so that I could hear the music. And as to that tin of tea, I saved the used tea leaves by wrapping them in a linen towel. You never knew when they might come in handy after the tin ran out.

I also was in charge of handling coats and hats, although many guests kept their coats on or put them over their knees. And I was to recognize everyone who entered. There always was the worry that an NSBer, or worse, a plain-clothes Nazi, might come in and

79

betray or arrest my parents. In addition to the raised piano lid, my mother had fashioned a translucent curtain across the front window, to reduce the chances that anyone could see in from any angle.

As a matter of routine I kept an eye on the street. A *razzia* on such a Sunday afternoon would have been a disaster, although most of the audience was old; but my parents would have been in numerous violations without time for my father to hide. However, *razzias* were becoming rarer, and the Nazis seemed to be more intent on defensive preparations and the theft of remaining items such as bicycles and carts than in arresting people. But one afternoon in mid-January something alarming happened. One of my favourite pieces was the Beethoven 'Spring' Sonata for violin and piano, and I stood near the front door, listening to the final movement, when I glanced out and saw a German officer, obviously of high rank, standing right in front of the house. For a moment I thought that he might have merely heard the music and would soon move on, but he remained where he was. I heard the last few bars of the movement approaching and knew that applause would follow, so I quickly walked into the living room, held up both arms, and whispered to my mother that a Nazi was standing outside.

My father quickly explained the situation, and my mother immediately began to play a Mozart sonata; no one should leave the house until the coast was clear.

But the officer stood there, and while my mother played, my father went to people individually and advised them to leave via the back door and through the gardens of the Ladies Bakker and Mr Richter. The music continued, and people left calmly. The slow departure seemed to be working. It was just as well, because the dusk curfew would soon begin.

When everyone was out of the house, the kitchen door had closed for the last time and the music could stop, we heaved a sigh of relief. Whatever happened next, the illegal gathering had been dispersed, no names had been taken and there had been no incident. Surely, we thought, the German would now move on.

We were mistaken. The officer walked up to our front door and rang the bell. My mother opened the small window in the upper part of the door; it was dark now, and we had no lights.

'*Guten Abend*,' he said in cultured German. 'I have listened with admiration to your music making. I see you had a little crowd here! May I come in?'

I stood at the back of the hallway, near the kitchen, and could sense that my mother was shaken. In any case, no one could refuse a Nazi entry into one's house, so she opened the door and he stepped inside. He took off his cap, which had an impressive insignia on it, and his heavy green overcoat. He wore a uniform with leather straps, shiny buttons, a large revolver in a holster, and tall, shiny black leather boots.

'My name is Weidling,' he said. 'I and my staff have just been assigned to administer Soestdijk and environs. I am also a music lover. I like to sing operatic arias. Can we sit down and discuss this?'

As he talked, he invited himself into the nearly dark living room, where the chairs of the audience still stood as I had arranged them. My father, who had listened to the conversation from the top of the stairs, now came down and introduced himself, unsmiling.

'You truly are an excellent duo,' said Weidling. 'I would enjoy coming to your concerts. I would also enjoy making music with you.'

'Unfortunately,' my father said, 'we are no longer doing the concerts. This was the last. And as you can see, we have no lights. Obviously we cannot play in the dark, and of course there is no time during the daylight hours.'

'Well, there is always Saturday,' the German said. 'And I can bring a carbide lamp with me from headquarters, if we must play in the evening.'

'But what about the music, the scores?' my mother asked. 'We do not have any operatic music. We have only piano and violin music.'

'But I have the music,' Weidling said. 'I carry it with me always, everywhere. By the way, you must have had quite a number of people here this afternoon.'

There was no mistaking the critical content of the moment, and even I understood it. My parents could not refuse Weidling outright without endangering our lives. But by agreeing, we would

81

soon be suspected of collaboration. That could be fatal too. The German, however, left no options for the time being.

'I will be here on Tuesday evening, with lights to play by and with music to play from.'

'Please bring some food as well,' my mother said. 'I would have nothing to offer you.'

The officer put on his coat and cap and left, bowing and kissing my mother's hand. It was an ominous moment. We walked into the kitchen and my father lit our only source of light, a contraption that suspended a cotton thread into a layer of oil floating on top of some water in a glass. We sat at the table and my parents talked. There was no solution. I felt somehow betrayed: how could that glorious music lead to this dreadful dilemma? Already the nights were long and cold, I was always hungry, and now our future seemed in doubt in a new and frightening way.

On Tuesday evening, Weidling appeared, bringing not only his carbide lamp and sheet music, but also a bag full of food, including a whole loaf of bread. The carbide lamp produced a blindingly bright light; I had never seen anything like it. But within minutes of his turning it on, German soldiers banged loudly on our front door, threatening to shoot: the edges around our curtains violated the blackout regulations. My dad opened the door to be confronted by two belligerent Nazis who shouted orders to turn off the light. As my father tried to explain, the shouting got louder, and one of the officers pointed his rifle right at my dad's chest. Just then, officer Weidling, in his full regalia, appeared in the doorway. I caught a glimpse of one of the soldiers' faces. He looked as if he had seen a ghost.

And so the music started, Weidling singing from *La Bohème* and my mother and father providing accompaniment and ad hoc obbligato. He sang passably well, I thought, very loudly and with much emotion; but what a sight this was, my diminutive mother sitting at the piano, my father standing next to her, reading from the score, and a corpulent German officer in full uniform singing his heart out. I went to the kitchen and used some firewood to boil a kettle of water, so my mother would be able to serve tea when the music was over. When it was, Weidling sat down to talk about his family in Dresden, and of the course the war was taking. He could not understand, he said, the vehemence of Dutch hatred for the Germans. Did we not have much in common? My dad described what had happened in the village during successive Nazi regimes. The conversation got loud, and dangerously candid. If Weidling were to come back, would he please wear civilian clothes? That would not be possible, Weidling said. But he understood the problems he might cause and would be discreet: 'Anything for music!'

But he was to be anything but discreet. When he came again, a week later, he brought with him an officer named Lukas. I cannot remember Lukas's rank, but I do remember the fear he caused. Weidling was a German officer of high rank doing his job; Lukas was an angry, brooding, vindictive Nazi. Weidling wanted to sing and talk; Lukas wanted to ask my father questions about his status. I felt sure that Lukas would demand to see my father's identity papers, that very night. Fortunately that did not happen, but Lukas would check some files at headquarters. We were surely heading for disaster.

Good fortune, however, blessed my parents. The next, and last, time we saw Weidling and Lukas, no music was played. It was two days after the first wave of attacks by Allied bombers on the German city of Dresden in mid-February 1945. News of the attacks had just reached the two Germans, both of whom had families there. It was a tense, difficult evening. Lukas seemed to be the sort of Nazi who could order the extermination of an entire village, as had happened at Putten. The two officers came to talk about their fears for Dresden, but we feared Lukas and we expected to hear from him again, and not as a social guest. But a few days later, Weidling and his staff were reassigned and a new German regime settled into their headquarters. We never heard from them again.

Still, this episode spelled the end of the house concerts. The risk was too great. And my parents' energies were dwindling. As any musician knows, performing is a physically as well as mentally demanding task, and a full-length concert requires more than a nearly empty stomach. So those stimulating Sundays ended, as did the modest flow of sustenance they had generated. Now we really were on our own.

8

SURVIVAL

The dark, cold winter of 1945 wore on mercilessly. The prospect of liberation had receded; we seemed rarely to talk about it any more. My father had more or less given up on his map. Food was running out despite my mother's stringent rationing. Our cellar supply of fruit and nuts would not last much longer. We had consumed the last of the rancid pig's meat. The cold was numbing. Frost flowers covered most of the windows of the house. Despite my father's best efforts, water pipes froze and repairs were out of the question. There was a tin of paraffin, with which he kept a flame going in the downstairs WC. The upstairs bathroom was of no use. Personal hygiene became a low priority.

The potato-peel soup from the village distribution centre became critical to our diet. I was the one sent to trade our coupons for soup, and I found a way to beat the system by carefully folding the coupons so that the cashier would mistake the number and take only part of our allotment. By getting in the queue at dawn, I could bring the first panful home and then return quickly to queue up again for a second helping. But getting the soup home sometimes was easier said than done. People leaving the kitchen, especially older people and youngsters like me, were often attacked on the way home. One day, a fight over a pan of soup erupted just ahead of me. Had I been walking in front of, rather than behind, the boy who was attacked, I would have been the victim. During the fight, the pan of soup spilled in the gutter. As I hurried past, both parties tried to scoop up, by hand, what now lay in the street. The owner of the pan tried to put some soup back in it. The attacker ate what he scooped up. When I described the incident to my mother, she burst into tears. 'We are reduced to fighting among ourselves and to eating from the gutter,' she cried. 'What will become of us?'

In fact, we villagers could be rather cruel to each other despite our mutual misfortune. I found that out when my clothes and shoes began to run out, and I was compelled to wear makeshift clothing. I was not gaining much weight, but I was growing, and my shoes and winter coat no longer fitted. My mother had a fur coat, and one day when deep snow covered the road to Baarn, she told me to wear it: keeping warm was more important than how one looked. But at school I got a merciless taunting from my class-mates, and I realized that how you looked did matter. As it was, it soon did not matter. School attendance was shrinking for reasons of danger, hunger, illness. In midwinter Mr van Dijk announced that classes were 'suspended'.

I should have known better when it came to shoes, but when one of my two pairs had worn out completely and the other was too small, my mother told me to try one of her low-heel, still usable pairs. I did, and they turned out to be wearable, but they looked like girl's shoes to me. Not so, said my mother; and at least my feet would be dry. But all I had to do was to appear on the street with them. Before long I was surrounded by laughing, pointing kids. So much for those dry feet.

My time outside was dwindling anyway. I had little energy to play; walking Bobby had not been my responsibility for some time. The winter days were short. I shovelled snow when neces-sary and sometimes went across the street, but otherwise I spent my time in the kitchen or the music room, often with Bobby by my side.

My parents created a routine to help keep our spirits up. My mother always managed to put some small amount of food on the table in the late afternoon; we sat down to eat before it got totally dark. Then my dad would light a floating-wick contraption using his paraffin supply, and we would sing canons and other songs. From '*Vader Jacob*' ('Frère Jacques') to 'It's a Long Way to Tipperary' and 'Smile the While', we sang our hearts out, and our repertoire grew as the winter wore on. My mother, I realized, had a wonderful, clear voice. Many years later I learned that someone who had heard her sing a solo at her music school had offered to pay for her entire further education and training in music, on condition that she would make singing, rather than the piano, her career. But she preferred to continue with her piano.

In the near-darkness we would sing until about half past eight, and then we went upstairs to the music room, now serving as our shared bedroom too. At the foot of my parents' beds stood a table with three chairs; my bed was against the opposite wall. Before going to bed, my father put his light on the table and read aloud from a series of books. By the flickering flame in the glass we sat at the table, my dad reading about the history of Dutch exploration around the North Cape, about Dutch sailors marooned on Arctic islands and their desperate efforts to survive the northern winter. When the ice closed in on them, one story went, they dismantled their ship and built shelters from the timbers and sail, knowing that, barring a miracle, their hope of ever leaving the island alive was gone. All they could do now was to try to prolong their lives, even in this most terrible, freezing environment. What, I thought after each chapter, did I have to complain about? The house was cold, but no blizzard tore through it. We were awfully hungry, but every day there seemed to be something to eat. And surely the war would be over, sooner or later. We did have hope, unlike those heroic explorers.

My days of confinement were also eased by my parents' large and varied library. I loved to read, and in that library I found adventure books, history books, picture books and atlases. It was a gold mine, and it kept me busy for days. I liked travel books the most, especially when the descriptions of distant journeys were accompanied by maps. If they were not, I got the atlas and traced them myself. At the table in the kitchen I took imaginary travels to faraway countries and envisioned places where it was always warm, where food was ample, and where you would be safe.

One particular book became a favourite, and I read it over and over again. It was written by a geographer named Hendrik Willem van Loon, and it described life as he saw it in what was then still the Dutch East Indies, now Indonesia. His vivid and admiring

86

Rotterdam, May 1940. The tower of the St. Laurens church somehow withstood the bombing, and served as a beacon of survival throughout the war. (Photographs of Rotterdam by my uncle, A. Erwich)

The soaring roof, magnificent interior and superb glasswork of the St. Laurens church were totally destroyed. The church was restored after the war.

The elegant Witte de Wit Street, one of Rotterdam's most fashionable avenues, was ruined.

The historic (left) as well as modern wings of Rotterdam's City Hall took direct hits, but no fires broke out here and the buildings could be repaired.

There was much loss of life at the Weimar Hotel, where fires raged after the bombs struck.

The damage at Wolfshoek, a mixed industrial and residential area, was enormous, but several of the river boats, loading cargo when the *Luftwaffe* struck, stayed afloat.

The house at Julianalaan (later Louise de Colignylaan) 1, Soestdijk in the late summer of 1941.

With my father, mother, and Bobby in the back garden, spring 1942.

nu de aardap-
pels van de boot
halen dat was
tamelyk gauw
gedaan
vader heeft het
stuur van zyn
fiets gebroken
naar wy zijn
nog eens gewoon
naar spakenburg
geweest om te
ruilen platzat
zyn we huiswaarts
gekeerd
ik had zoo'n honger
dat ik langs de deur
een boterham
gevraagd heb

A page from my wartime diary. It refers to potatoes my mother had put on a boat during her hunger march and to a trip for barter (*ruilen*) at Spakenburg. The last line: 'I was so hungry that I went door to door to ask for a slice of bread'.

The *Viersprong* in the late 1930's. Straight ahead is the Wilhelminalaan leading up to the Lazarusberg; the Julianalaan forks to the left just beyond the group of trees at the centre of the photograph.

The *Viersprong* on a summer day just before the war, probably August 1939.

A clandestine photograph of the *Viersprong* just after the explosives have gone off and fire erupts from the upper vestibule. Courtesy of the Soester Museum.

The roof collapses as fire engulfs the lower floor. The blast has scattered glass in all directions and already prisoners are sweeping the street. Courtesy of the Soester Museum.

On May 6, 1945, Soestdijk's townspeople erected a poetic sign above the commemorative plaque giving the date of the Viersprong's destruction: 'What through capricious terror and brute force was destroyed will in freedom be restored.' But it was not to be. The still-windowless house of the vet, Dr. Kok, is in the background. Courtesy of the Soester Museum.

descriptions of landscapes and towns, customs and traditions, weather and climate, food and drink transported me to sun-drenched, palm-lined islands where people were gracious and life was good. The author, I read, was a geographer, and this book showed the way a geographer looked at the world.

I followed van Loon on his walks through dripping rainforests where danger lurked at every turn, his climbs of volcanic mountains where the ground shook underfoot, his visits to teeming cities where the streets were 'rivers of humanity'. His powers of observation were amazing; from the deck of a fishing boat crossing between two islands he saw more than I could imagine. At school my geography lessons had confined themselves to the Netherlands, and I liked the maps and pictures of our provinces. But that was nothing compared to van Loon's kind of geography. His book opened windows to the world.

So I searched for other references to geography in the library. The encyclopedia entry under this rubric seemed dull and technical compared to what I had just read; it was mostly about the study of rivers and soils and 'the physical world', as the column described it. A few references to the 'study of peoples' hardly matched the vibrant narratives in van Loon's geography of the Indies. Nor did the encyclopedia article say anything about how you became a geographer. And what did geographers do, other than writing and teaching?

But for the moment I wanted to read more about *aardrijkskunde* (earth-realm-knowledge), as geography was called in Dutch. More recently the term *geografie* has also come unto use, but the best-known Dutch academic-geographic society continues to be known as the *Koningklijk Nederlands Aardrijkskundig Genootschap* (KNAG), the Royal Netherlands Geographic Association. One of the books I found in the library dealt with peoples living in particular environments: Pygmies in the African rainforest, Tuaregs in the desert, Eskimos in the Arctic, Tibetans in the frosty Asian highlands. Like those Dutch pioneers marooned on that island north of Siberia, these people had to contend with environments that seemed to make every day a battle for survival. I wouldn't last a day in the forest or in the desert. But at school I had learned that the Dutch, too, had coped with great environmental danger. Much of our country lay below sea level, and the system of dikes and pumps that kept cities dry and polders safe for crops and cattle also was a remarkable adaptation to a threatening environment. And nature had dealt the Netherlands some deathly blows over the centuries as storms caused dikes to fail and floods killed thousands. I wondered whether the Germans would breach the dikes of our province deliberately, if they were about to lose the war. Well, we would be safe on an upper floor.

The teachers at the Nieuwe Baarnse School had encouraged an activity I really liked, and which turned out to have a geographic dimension: stamp collecting and trading. My parents promoted it and gave me stamps their friends had, and when there still was mail, Sja sometimes sent me foreign stamps. For my seventh birthday they gave me a used, thick stamp album that still contained some of the previous owner's entries. By sometimes spending a few pennies of pocket money and by careful trading, I had built a collection of over 500 stamps. Now I found a book in my parents' library that dealt with the history and geography of stamps. Its author urged stamp collectors to do more than merely assemble stamps: they should also be carefully examined for what they revealed. Some stamps, for example, display miniature maps and when this is the case, the countries that issue them may be making a point. To illustrate, the author enlarged two stamps, one from Chile and the other from Argentina, showing the same part of Antarctica as belonging to each of them. When you see a map on a stamp, he said, get a magnifying glass and see if it matches your atlas map. If not, the issuing country probably is making a geopolitical point.

I had not seen this word – geopolitical – before, but *geopolitiek* seemed to summarize what we were going through. Wasn't my father's red-shaded map an illustration of the geography of strategy, of geopolitics? And those frightening maps of the *sperrgebiete*? I got my school geography book from my room, but there was nothing in it about this. Names, places, products, roads and railways seemed to be all my textbook was about. But from van Loon and from that book about stamps I could see that geography had many other aspects. In those days it carried me away from the daily problems, the isolation, the cold, the hunger. I

88

was in my tenth year, with no prospect of ever seeing what van Loon did. But I wanted to learn to see the world through his geographer's eyes. These final months of the war set me on a life-long course.

By mid-March the food situation had become critical. The basement hoard had run out. My father, who normally weighed about 75 kilos was down to 60 and showed symptoms of starvation. My mother weighed less than 50 kilos. For the first time I was losing weight and strength. From neighbours we heard tragic and fearsome stories of people in the village dying for lack of food, especially oldsters, and others too weak to move.

The refugee influx that escalated after the lost battle for Arnhem made things worse, and now hundreds of outsiders were arriving from the direction of The Hague and Amsterdam. The authorities forced local residents to take in many of these people. Some were genuine refugees, destitute and dislocated, but others, it seemed, were opportunists, scavengers, or worse. The vet, Dr Kok, took in a thickset bearded man who said that he was a professor of linguistics, and his wife. He alleged that he could converse in more than 20 languages, and soon had befriended the Batenburgs. Frequently he sat with us in Noud's room, but no one ever dared ask him to demonstrate his linguistic skills. He turned out to be a crook, and the Koks were lucky that minor theft was all that befell them. The couple who moved in with old Mr and Mrs Richter seemed nice enough though very reclusive, but it turned out that they were determined to occupy an entire floor of his house not only during, but after the war as well. The Ladies Bakker were fortunate. Their attic room was taken by an old, distinguished couple. The husband had been captain of a large ship and had met with a serious accident in the engine room, losing the full use of his left arm and hand. Although not in good health he managed well, and when he discovered that I collected stamps he often had me over to trade – which really meant giving me stamps I could never afford.

With the help of Mr Batenburg my mother had managed to defer our having to take in lodgers, but this could end any day. Meanwhile, all these people further strained the food situation in the village. The twice-weekly potato-peel soup ration, even when

I managed to double it, was not enough to keep us alive. Other families were in the same situation, and my mother got word that some of the women in the village who still had the strength were undertaking so-called 'hunger marches', riding their bikes or walking still available carts (even prams) to the farm country around Zwolle, about 65 kilometres to the north-east. There they would ask for, and sometimes beg for, food of any kind, and bring it back to the village. Women would go in groups, sometimes in pairs. They took a considerable risk, because they would have to be able to feed themselves if they were to have the strength to make it back.

I was unaware that my parents had decided that my mother should go, but I remember my father working on her bicycle the previous Sunday evening. Although the Nazis had confiscated virtually all men's bikes, and most bicycle tyres had gone flat in any case, many women's bikes were still in citizens' hands. My mother was fortunate: she had one so-called 'massive' tyre (a solid rubber strap round the wheel) in the rear and a real, still serviceable tyre, on the front wheel. Many cyclists rode on the metal rims, which was dangerous as well as uncomfortable, and the wheels eventually failed. My dad helped her strap a blanket for sleeping on the luggage holder, plus several canvas bags for any food she might secure.

I write as if I saw her depart, but I did not. She left at dawn on Monday morning and did not wake me up; she could not bear to say farewell to me. The trip would be dangerous, and some of the women who had gone north had not come back. When I got up, my father explained why she was not home, and that he could not tell me when she would be back. But when she did return, she might have food for all of us. That day, when I was across the street, Mrs Batenburg said that the whole family was praying for my mother.

Now began the longest, slowest days of the war. My mother was the steady rock throughout all our troubles; she was always there. Despite everything she would sing in the kitchen, talk to Bobby, play her piano. Now the house was eerily quiet. My father, I sensed, doubted the wisdom of my mother's odyssey, and he seemed somehow diminished by her absence. When it got dark and even colder than the day had been, I wondered where she was, whether she had a place to sleep, something to eat. What if she had an accident and needed help? And if she did find food, what were her chances of actually reaching home safely with it, given the frequency of robberies? Even Bobby, for all her spunk and spirit, now a tiny body of skin and bones, seemed to wilt. We had resolved to stay together in the event of my father being taken by the Germans and marched away; and now we were separated after all. Was this a mistake?

Nothing seemed to make the hours go by. I could not concentrate on anything. My father tried to give me a daily violin lesson, and he proposed that we prepare a duo with which to surprise her upon her return. I worked on it, but my heart was not in it, and anyway, trying to play the violin in this awful cold was hardly worth it. Sitting down with a book only meant getting up to walk to the window. Time seemed to have slowed to a crawl.

The worst of it was that there was no way to make contact. By midweek we calculated that my mother would be in the environs of Zwolle now, probably knocking on farmers' doors. On Friday I began sitting at the window, looking down the street for her, because this was the first day she might conceivably be back. When I went to bed on Saturday night, I knew I would not sleep, nor did my father. She had been gone for six days, and most women had come back in less time than that.

And then, on Sunday morning, I was sitting in the music room with Bobby when she suddenly sat bolt upright and began barking. I looked out of the front window but saw nothing, but Bobby ran downstairs to the front door, almost tumbling down the steps. I ran down and opened the door just as I heard the clang of the garden gate – and there was my mother, pushing a bicycle loaded with bulging bags of produce. She looked dreadful, her hair tousled, her clothes rumpled and streaked with what looked like mud, her shoes caked with dirt. But she had succeeded. The bags we unloaded in the kitchen contained potatoes, turnips, carrots, beans, butter, cheese, bread, even a small bottle of milk, almost unimaginable luxuries all. In truth it was less than one weekly supermarket purchase for an average family during peacetime, but carefully rationed this would last us for many days longer. I have never forgotten that moment and recall it almost every time we load our groceries into the car.

My father got a fire going and heated water in several pans for my mother to use in the bathroom. Meanwhile we waited to hear her story. The road to Zwolle had been packed with people pushing bikes and other vehicles, looking for food. Knocking on farmhouse doors and asking for food was difficult, but she had got used to it. Some farmers were very kind; others pointed to the water pump and said 'help yourself'. The farther you went from the main road, the nicer the farmers seemed to be. Some even had a system to ration what they had available to the hunger marchers. But going on the back roads made the journey longer, and she and her friends had become very tired. She had slept in a barn with the animals, in an attic, in a refugee shelter. They had just crossed a bridge when a plane strafed the adjacent railway line. At another bridge there was a German checkpoint and she had to report everything she had; whatever she missed in her accounting would not be allowed to pass. She had been propositioned by Nazi soldiers, and threatened with confiscation of all she had. Her bike was too heavily loaded to ride it, so she had walked throughout the previous day and night.

I was enormously proud of her. She had risked so much to save us all, and she was so matter-of-fact about it. 'She is my hero,' I wrote in my diary. She truly was the strongest of the three of us, and as long as she was well, all would be well.

The next several days allowed us a glimpse of what life would be like after the end of the war, when there would be food for today, tomorrow, and for the foreseeable future. My mother cooked meals with potatoes and vegetables and a sauce she concocted from onions and turnips, and for a few wonderful days our hunger receded. We sliced the dark, almost wet wholewheat bread ('real farmer's bread,' my father said) thinly so that it would last over as many days as possible. Our kitchen table looked to me like a banquet. Even Bobby got a few scraps.

Outside, the winter wore on relentlessly. Our small flock of chickens in their run at the far end of the back garden was down to one survivor, but the eggs she laid in the hen house were precious to us. While things were better, my mother would throw bread crumbs into the run, but now we collected even those and put them in the soup from the soup kitchen. My dad opened the gate to the run so our egg-layer could forage over a wider area, but in truth the frozen ground had little to offer. But obviously she had not forgotten where those breadcrumbs came from. Soon she was sitting on the empty flower box, looking in and pecking at the kitchen window. I wondered if, under her coat of feathers, she was as underweight as we were. Certainly her egg production had dropped off.

I was surprised that Bobby never attacked her. But at times they were both scurrying in the garden, without any tussles. A routine developed: almost as soon as we came to the kitchen in the morning, the window-pecking would start. When we left, she would go into the garden. At night she slept in the hen house. I wondered if she would ever realize that her pecking on the window produced no results. She probably dreamed of buckets of grain just as we did of meat and potatoes.

L ife in the village now took on an unreal, almost perverse quality. It was early spring now, but the cold of the Hunger Winter hung on. Yet there was hope: we heard that the Allies were closing in on us from the south, east and even north-east. Liberation, according to some, was just days away. But all around us was evidence that the Nazis were planning to defend their hold over our village and its environs. They were digging manholes and trenches along the road beside the palace and along the Amsterdam road as well. They were making large, movable trellises wrapped in layers of barbed wire, and stacking them at key intersections. They also cut gaping triangular sections out of the huge old trees that still lined the village streets, so that these could be toppled instantly during an Allied advance. And they commandeered houses deemed to lie in strategic locations, summarily ousting their occupants.

There was no more fear of *razzias*; the search for Dutch men had stopped. On the other hand, German soldiers still policed the streets. And the proclamation and enforcement of *sperrgebiete* continued, making it risky to walk almost anywhere. Meanwhile, the Nazis were emptying and destroying their palace headquarters. Typewriters, adding machines, filing cabinets and office furniture lay in the street, hacked to pieces, or were thrown in the canal. Some German personnel were reported to be taking money for undamaged or slightly damaged office equipment. German troops were arriving in retreat, walking in groups and out of step, to be accommodated in the palace. I remembered those tightly packed columns I had seen entering Rotterdam, marching meticulously in step and singing vigorously, their shiny boots moving as one, their uniforms pressed and creased. This was quite a different scene. All that discipline was fleeting, after all.

In some ways it was safer to go outside again in the daytime, but now a new danger arose. The advancing Allies were tightening the noose from all directions, and the growing number of German soldiers and their weapons made attractive targets. Single-engined *jagers* (hunters), as we called them, patrolled the skies and strafed the enemy wherever he came into view, and it was always best not to be in the street when a Nazi column was passing. 'We'll be in artillery range soon,' my dad said. 'That may be more risky than those *jagers*.'

The *sperrzeit*, however, now seemed to pose less of a threat, because it was less effectively policed. On many evenings my father would check up and down the street for German soldiers, and then we would dash across to the Batenburgs to gather in Noud's room. Noud by now was very ill, unable to move his arms but still capable of participating in the conversation. His room had a south-facing window that could not be seen from the street, and when we sat in the dark the curtains were open.

For some time we had seen strange, thin trails of white smoke rising almost vertically into the sky, originating, it seemed, not much more than 30 kilometres away. In the afternoon sun such trails seemed to emanate from a small black projectile that soon raced out of sight. The trail hung in the air for some time after the launch. At night, through Noud's window; we would see a small flame rising in the same way, obviously from the same source.

We had heard that the Nazis had developed a 'miracle' weapon that would yet turn the tide of war, and while none of us believed this, the trails and flames gave us pause. We heard of great damage being inflicted on London and other English targets, and we learned that the weapons causing it were the V-l and the V-2. What we were seeing was the launching of these killer rockets. Apparently the launching facilities were mobile, for as the war front crept closer to us, so did the launches. Soon we were able, in the daytime, to distinguish between a low-angle launch and a nearly vertical one.

One evening we sat in Noud's room and heard the put-put of an engine that obviously was not that of aeroplane. It started about eight thirty, disappeared into the night, then came back again. We looked out of Noud's window and saw the irregular flicker of what looked like a flaming exhaust, illuminating a small, squat missile with short wings and an elevated tail. When it returned a third time, it was obvious what had happened: this was one of the V weapons, its steering mechanism malfunctioning, and it would crash and explode somewhere along its circular route. My dad's suggestion that we go to the basement when next we heard it was greeted with laughter, but I agreed. Certainly the conversation stopped dead when the noise started again, but after this fourth pass over us, there were no more returns. The next day my dad got a message that the V-l had come down not far from Hilversum around 10.15 p.m., its explosion killing one person and leaving a huge crater. He had been right. We took a chance.

On a mild late afternoon in early April, I was bouncing a ball off a wall in our back garden when one of the Batenburgs' daughters, Tilly, came round the corner of the house. 'Come, please,' she said quietly to my mother, who had seen her pass and opened the kitchen door. 'He is asking for you.' My mother went inside to get a scarf. Tilly turned to me and whispered, 'Noud is dying.' Then they hurried off. I leaned against the wall and thought for a moment about all those wartime evenings in Noud's room. He had survived the worst of times, and now his life was ebbing just as we prepared for the best.

Noud died in the late evening, and my mother kept the vigil with the Batenburg family. She was unable to return home that night as the curfew time had passed and crossing the street was too dangerous now to contemplate. The next day we filed past his body, his good looks still there. 'The Nazis still wouldn't believe it,' Jaap said bitterly.

Mr Batenburg told him to be quiet. 'He missed the end of the war, but he is free before us,' he said.

The Allied attacks on German targets in our area continued. Two days after Noud's death we could see a wave of dive-bombers attacking an ammunition depot in Amersfoort, a large town about 10 kilometres away. It was a fantastic sight, visible from the back bedroom. The planes would form a circle, and then, engines whining at high pitch, dive nearly vertically towards their objective. We were close enough so that you could see the bombs separating from the warplanes and see the flash of the explosions; the sound would reach us shortly after. Over and over again the attackers dived, eventually leaving huge clouds of smoke rising over the area. Then they left in formation, but the explosions continued far into the night. Our roof, like that in Schiedam, had a small skylight, and from a stepladder we could see what was happening. An ammunition train had been hit, and it was burning; wagonload after wagonload of ammunition blew up as the flames reached them. Thunderous blasts lit the columns of smoke from previous explosions. It was a fireworks display reminiscent of Rotterdam.

None of this, however, seemed to bring the war's end any closer. By mid-April, we were critically short of food. My mother's hoard from the hunger march was gone, no more fruits or nuts remained, and the soup kitchen had ceased operations. My father's forehead had taken on a bluish tinge and his eyes were so deeply set into their sockets that I thought his head looked like a skull. I was, in my mother's words, thin as a reed. It was cold again, and I had no energy.

In the third week of April a new threat arose. A shell, apparently launched from Allied lines near Amersfoort, fell on a house up the street from us and destroyed it. The next day two other shells landed harmlessly on empty sites. It was clear that we risked becoming the last battleground, and my father decided that we would move into the cellar beneath the kitchen, at least during the night, when no sirens would sound before the shells landed. Of course there always was the briefest of warnings: the bombs made a sharp whistling sound just before they exploded. But that was not enough to take cover. So my parents moved some valuables downstairs, laid some oriental rugs on the floor of the 3-metre square cellar, and put our bedding on top. I felt terribly uncomfortable: no heat, virtually no food, and no familiar bed.

Now our living space was reduced to the kitchen, the lavatory in the downstairs hallway, and the cellar. I wondered how necessary our cellar-dwelling was. Bombs whistled past fairly frequently, but the only house in our immediate neighbourhood that had been hit was the one up the street. But my father was adamant, and in any case the rest of the house was freezing. So I started reading my van Loon geography one more time, trying to believe that all this would bring the end of the war.

One casualty of our situation was the news. No one brought my father any information; we did not know what was happening even in our own area. But the contradictions continued. On 24 April, when the German defeat must have been obvious to all but the blindest Nazis, soldiers nailed another 'order' to the telephone pole across from our house. As of that date, Soestdijk and Baarn were declared *sperrgebiete*, and residents were allowed outside their houses only from 8 to 9 a.m. and from 5 to 6 p.m. 'Those who disobey, or appear to want to do so, will be shot without warning', the order stated. It hardly mattered. We were not leaving the house for other reasons.

A few days later something awful had to be done. We were desperate for food and my father decided that our chicken must be killed and eaten. It may seem strange that this would upset us all, but it did; somehow her presence at the kitchen window had become part of our daily lives and I think we all hoped that she, too, would survive the war. But it was not to be. My father asked a man who did gardening for the Batenburgs, and who sometimes managed to bring them a rabbit or a bird, to do what was needed. That late afternoon he caught her in the back garden and after it was over gave us the dressed fowl. I was amazed at how small it was. My mother shed a tear as she boiled it that evening, but we all knew there was no choice. We ate for four days from that chicken, and the soup my mother made from the bones lasted even longer.

F or some weeks before we began sleeping in the cellar, we had noticed that Bobby looked, somehow, deformed, all skin and bones but with a heavy belly. Since we saw the same in many children in the village, we assumed that she was simply showing signs of malnutrition. It was inconceivable that she could be pregnant in her condition – but she was. And while she was alone upstairs in the kitchen, where years earlier I had built her a corner doghouse, and we slept in the cellar, she had five puppies. My mother shouted the news when she was first to go upstairs one morning. Bobby lay protectively in her house under the corner table, and the tiny puppies looked like mice. I wanted to bring them all downstairs, but it was impossible. So I listened to her at night, walking about on the floor above. If *we* were hungry, I thought, how must she feel?

Outside, the Germans continued fortifying our area. The magnificent old oak, beech and pine trees they had partially carved now were given the *coup de grâce* and fell across the roadways. In one late April day the green canopies of Soestdijk were gone for ever. The barbed-wire barriers were pulled across intersections. The Nazis clearly were preparing for a house-to-house defence of the village. They set up an anti-aircraft battery right behind Stam's garage, not more than 40 metres from our kitchen door.

But during the first days of May there was less, rather than more, indication that combat was imminent. The bombardment to which we had become accustomed seemed to have abated. We did continue to sleep in the cellar, but we spent almost all our time upstairs during daylight hours. Spring had arrived, the sun warmed rooms we had long abandoned, the air was milder. Bobby mothered her puppies on I knew not what. She went outside to scavenge, but she was never gone for long. Here, I thought, was new life when so much of it was being lost. But there was nothing I could do to help her, except give her comfort.

Once again, however, we were virtually out of food. The soup kitchen no longer functioned, supply lines were broken, the rationing system had long since failed, and we were down to a few hundred calories a day. But now there were rumours that the Allies and the Germans were negotiating routes and sites for air drops of emergency provisions. 'It had better happen soon,' my father said. He looked terrible, his cheekbones protruding, his arms thin as rail, his clothes much too large for his shrinking frame. It had never occurred to me that it could actually happen, but he seemed to be failing now. He had no energy, no spark.

On the evening of 4 May 1945, nearly 11 months after D-Day, we were sitting in the kitchen at dusk when I saw Jaap, one of the Batenburg sons, running past the window. Loud banging on the door followed. My mother opened it, and a breathless Jaap pushed inside. 'They have capitulated!' he shouted. 'It's over! The *verdomde* (damned) Nazis have given up! We're free!' He was so full of excitement that he kept wiping his feet on the mat in front of the kitchen door, like a dog that had just done its business. We hugged each other and my father shook Jaap's hand. When would the Allies reach us? No one yet knew, said Jaap, but the official capitulation would be posted tomorrow. He wiped his feet again. 'Got to tell the Richters and the Bakkers,' he said, and on his way he went.

For some time we sat in silence in the gathering darkness, all of us deep in thought. Was this true? Might this be a trick? How reliable was Jaap's information? My father admonished us to be careful. 'Until you see Allied uniforms on our streets, don't take any chances. If it's true, there will be some angry Nazis around.' We decided to sleep upstairs, but for me sleep was impossible. I sat at the window, hoping to see the first Allied soldiers in the village, went to bed again, got up again. Was all this a dream?

At the first light of dawn I got dressed and went to the upstairs bathroom, from whose window I had seen Operation Bodenplatte five months earlier. Now I saw something even more unbelievable: from the tower of the Catholic church protruded a pole, and from that pole hung a Dutch flag, the red, white and blue. I raced to the bedroom and roused my parents, who ran to the window. Now

99

we knew: it really was over, we had made it, and a new life lay before us. It had been just five days short of five years since that terrible day in Rotterdam, and ours was the very last part of the Netherlands to be liberated, but we had survived.

9

PEACE

There is a passage in Beethoven's 'Pastoral' Symphony that describes a tranquil rural scene disrupted by the passing of a violent storm. Gusts of wind, bolts of lightning, thunderclaps, pelting rain roil the countryside. If you listen carefully, you can detect a sequence of squalls in what is obviously a weather front sweeping across the landscape. Then the rampage ends and the music portrays a scene of peace and serenity. The air is calm. Birds emerge from hiding. The danger is past.

Whenever I hear that symphony, and I have listened to it countless times, I am reminded of those first post-war days in May 1945. All of us, I am sure, had expectations about liberation day, whenever it would come. Mine involved cheering crowds, marching bands, stirring speeches, late-night celebrations. But when it finally happened, those first days were mostly calm, quiet, even dull. There were Dutch tricolours on houses and public buildings, and there were people in the streets, but generally things were placid, serene. In truth, many of those people were too exhausted, hungry, even ill to celebrate boisterously. Still 5 May was not what I had imagined it would be.

But there were memorable moments. Some youngsters got a stepladder, tore down the Louise de Coligny street sign, and put up a piece of cardboard with Julianalaan printed on it. Up the Wilhelminalaan, just below the Lazarusberg, a crowd gathered around the house of a known NSB family; the townspeople confined them to their premises until the Allied authorities arrived. In the evening, we went to the Batenburg house, where the patriarch

of the family opened a bottle of wine kept, he said, for years await-
ing this occasion. But that gathering, too, was quiet and introspec-
tive. There was none of the jubilation of which I had dreamed so
often.

In any case, uninhibited celebration might be premature. Even
while Dutch flags flew everywhere, the Nazis still rode around in
their armoured cars. The Allied forces had not reached us yet.
Although they did not intervene (though there were rumours of
some flag-burning and intimidation) they still held the power.

For my father, the end of the war came just in time. He collapsed the day after our evening at the Batenburgs and was in bed
for several weeks, the first time I had ever seen him incapacitated.
Our doctor (a family friend who had patronised the house concerts) said that what he needed, simply, was sustenance. And supplies were arriving that very day in dramatic fashion: the Swedish
Air Force conducted a series of 'drops', parachuting crates of food
to several open fields in the area including, near us, the Eng. A distribution system had already been set up, and within 24 hours we
began receiving white bread, packets of flour, canned sausages,
tinned sardines and other provisions. Our doctor cautioned my
dad against eating too much too soon. 'Your system will have to
adapt to regular and complete meals,' he said.

I had all kinds of plans for the days ahead: I wanted to see my
old school and what the Nazis had done to it, wanted to bike to
Soesterberg and see the war damage. But a day later I was in bed
too, and would stay there, on and off, for six weeks. Once again
my mother was the strongest one! She moved my bed to the window so I could see what was happening in the street, but I was
jaundiced and without energy. Any excursions would have to be
put off.

Now the Allied forces began arriving, and with the windows
open I could hear the tanks, armoured vehicles, trucks, cannon and
other war equipment moving up the highway. Now the people
were out cheering and clapping their hands and waving at our
liberators. The Canadians were the first to reach us, and soon the
Canadian flag flew everywhere. Sick or not, I had to catch a
glimpse of this scene, and my mother helped me down to the corner. There I sat on one of the downed tree trunks and watched as

102

trucks full of soldiers giving the V sign received a heroes' welcome. People threw flowers and girls threw kisses and kids ran along the side of the road asking for handouts, and the generous Canadians threw chocolates, cigarettes, flag badges and other gifts to the crowd. It went on and on, a parade of armour and personnel that reached down the Amsterdam road as far as the eye could see, an endless stream of military power that finally proved that Nazi rule had ended.

And from my bed I could see much else. A band formed in the village and went around playing the national anthem and patriotic tunes, followed enthusiastically by a flag-waving, singing crowd. One of their first stops was right under my window, where the renamed Wilhelminalaan and Julianalaan intersected. People stood singing and saluting in the the little park where those machine-gun toting Nazis had appeared that frightening day. There was a ceremony at the Viersprong, where the people erected a board carrying a poem about destruction and reconstruction. And, lucky for me, the Canadians chose a large villa on the Wilhelminalaan as their local headquarters, so that suddenly the street across from my room was filled with activity. The Canadians rode around on huge motorbikes and wore impressive leather corsets (or so they looked) around the waist as they drove, often at breakneck speed, up and down the road. The pavement teemed with youngsters looking for souvenirs, and the friendly Canadians always had something to give away. Behind our house, kids were playing on the anti-aircraft battery the Germans had set up, rotating the platform and raising and lowering the gun barrels. Up the Amsterdam road, a cinema opened, called the City Theatre ('Kitty' in local parlance), and it showed war films in which the heroic Allies always won the day.

Repairs were going on everywhere. German soldiers, jeered by groups of bystanders, were cutting up the barbed-wire barricades they had constructed and filling the foxholes they had dug in their futile preparations for defence. But the great old trees they had downed, and were now sawing into pieces to be hauled away, could not be restored; our village would never look the same. Near the town hall, citizens had set up a makeshift barber's shop. There they cut the hair of women and girls who had consorted with the

Germans during the occupation, leaving them bald and mortified ('a small price to pay,' said my mother). And NSB families, having been held under house arrest by the citizens, were being taken away by the new Dutch authorities.

But in truth there seemed to be very little retaliation, perhaps because the people were exhausted by the Hunger Winter and its aftermath. Many of the people who had betrayed their country and their fellow Hollanders soon were back in society, holding good jobs and benefiting from reconstruction. Some found positions in orchestras; others joined university faculties. Of course many, after their initial incarceration, left the country for Argentina, South Africa and other destinations. The overwhelming majority got off easy.

Before I was back on my feet my father did something I had looked forward to for many months: he exhumed the old Royal Enfield. I watched from the rear bathroom window, and what a mess it was. Rotting paper, oily rags, wet soil, pieces of carpet – but out it came, covered in mud but still recognizably a motor-cycle! My dad hosed it off and wheeled it into the garage, and worked on it all day. By evening, he had cleaned it up, put some fuel in it and, incredibly, got it running. Even the tyres and the seats had survived; only the rubber of the passenger seat was a bit eroded. The silver trim of the fuel tank shone as it had before the burial. The next day, he rode it down to Stam's garage to show them that his gamble had paid off. It should, I thought, have been the stuff of an advertisement in one of those glossy magazines. A motorcycle would have to be well made to survive what this one had!

In late June I was well enough to start enjoying life again. And how my world had changed! Bobby's puppies were big enough to find new homes, and my mother was spreading the word. But we would keep one of them – the one that was always last, last to clamber over the edge of the kennel, last to the food, last in any race to the back fence. He was a lunk, and we gave him a fairly derogatory name, Loebas. But we loved him, and we thought that Bobby might enjoy the company.

104

I am not sure that Bobby agreed, but she never left any doubt as to who was boss in the kitchen. Even after Loebas grew larger than she was, Bobby would intimidate him, sometimes by a stare, sometimes by giving him a piece of her mind. Loebas seemed to accept his number-two status, although he did best her in one respect: being bigger, he could run faster. In the reopened Crown Domain he would lead his mother on many a relentless chase, staying just far enough ahead of her to keep her in yelping, angry pursuit.

And the village had returned to comparative normalcy. Many shops that had been closed for a long time (some for years) had reopened. The bookstore across from the City Theatre now displayed a wealth of new material ranging from illustrated volumes about the war to magazines and newspapers I had never seen. I well remember the moment when I picked up a copy of the *National Geographic Magazine* with its yellow border, fold-out maps and photographs in colour: there was that word *geography* again! It was the first time I saw in pictures what van Loon had described in words: a wonderful, amazing world. And all of it was geography! I had no doubt: when school started again, I would concentrate on this subject and make it mine.

Also in that bookstore was a stack of magazines about America. I sat on the floor and went through them page by page, marvelling at the pictures of city skylines and towering skyscrapers, bustling streets filled with cars and pedestrians, spectacular scenery from coastlines to canyons. 'America the Beautiful' was the title of one of the articles. I wrote the word 'beautiful' on a piece of paper and asked my mother what it meant. *Prachtig*, she said. I needed no convincing. If a land this beautiful could produce soldiers as nice as those in our village, all was well there in America. And I would somehow get there, to see it for myself.

My dad explained the difference between Americans and Canadians. Those good military men in our village were Canadians, not Americans. But I looked at the atlas map and saw that the whole continent was called North America. So Canadians were Americans too? North Americans, my dad corrected. To me it was all the same.

'Maybe they'll join some day,' my father said one evening at dinner. 'The United States and Canada have a lot in common, you know. Except for one Canadian province, almost everyone speaks English. And the cities and farms and ways of life are pretty much the same.' What prompted this discussion were the headlines of the week: the newspapers were reporting that the Netherlands, Belgium and Luxembourg were forming an economic union called Benelux. This had apparently been planned even before the end of the war, and now the scheme was becoming reality. 'Just imagine,' my dad said. 'You would be able to travel to Belgium and Luxembourg without going through customs, and sell your goods on the other side of the border.' And if it would work here, it might be an example to other countries, even Canada and the United States. Not all the Dutch newspapers were so enthused. I recall one 1945 headline: *Wij Krijgen de Benen, Zij Krijgen de Luxe!* (We get the bones, they get the luxuries!) said *De Groene Amsterdammer*. And soon Benelux was what my father called a 'political issue'. Political parties were active again for the first time in nearly six years, and Benelux was a major topic of debate. Some politicians said that we had just regained our sovereignty; now was not the time to begin yielding any of it. Others argued that by combining, even if only in the economic sphere, small countries like ours would be better off in the new Europe that lay ahead. I remember reading a column in *Elsevier* in which the author predicted that Benelux would be a forerunner for all of Western Europe. It was the first time I had seen the phrase United States of Europe in print. That notion was enough to send some politicians into oratorical orbit.

In truth, Holland's recovery was not going all that well. After the Swedish rescue missions and following the Allied takeover, there still were problems with food supply. No one was starving, but the amount and variety of food still was limited. And un-employment was high, leading quickly to social disorder. For the first time I heard my father and mother talking about 'commu-nists', politicians who would take advantage of the prevailing stagnation and who, like the occupying Nazis, had masters in another country. 'Stalin could be the next Hitler,' my father said. 'His henchmen are already here.'

Unlike some of his colleagues, however, my dad had no thought

106

of leaving the Netherlands – yet. When the position of concert master (leader) of the NCRV Chamber Orchestra in Hilversum became available, he auditioned, and from a huge pool of applicants he was appointed. Soon he was negotiating with the people at the Stam garage to buy an old Wolseley that had been stored there for years. And my mother's piano-teaching practice grew by leaps and bounds. The future looked bright.

I enjoyed those summer days wandering in the village and walking the dogs in the Crown Domain, but I knew that there was much catching up to do in school. In June, Mr van Dijk had informed parents of pupils at the Nieuwe Baarnse School that classes would resume at the villa while repairs were done at the school building, which had been ravaged by the Nazis. We were called back to school in midsummer, and in several weeks the school year that had been interrupted by the Hunger Winter came to an end. When we returned to the original school building, we all moved up to the next year, and I was in the fifth, Mr Vermeer's class.

And here was my chance: geography was one of the key topics in the fifth and sixth forms. This classroom had a large globe and a rack of wall maps, and I could hardly wait. But the textbook we were given, a slim volume by two geographers with the memorable names of Brummelkamp and Fahrenfort, turned out to be nothing like the writings of van Loon. Descriptions of towns and cities consisted of short paragraphs loaded with facts about the size of the population, the number of factories, the kinds of products, the destinations of exports. It was all pretty dull, and Mr Vermeer was not a particularly inspiring teacher.

And, as it turned out, geography class could generate a huge amount of homework. We had five hour-long classes a day, three in the morning and two in the afternoon. Every class yielded a batch of homework. Thank goodness for Wednesday afternoons, when there were no classes: then you could catch up with the inevitable backlog. But this geography class was the worst of all. Not only did you have to complete the homework, but you had to know it by heart for the next class.

Our first exercise had to do with Dutch cities. On one page there was a map showing major cities and towns in the two provinces of North and South Holland, all labelled. On the following page was the same map, but without the names. Our homework for that first evening was not only to label all cities and towns on the blank map, but also to learn to do that again, without referring to the first map.

I sat at the dining room table that evening, trying to learn the place names but without success. My father came by and saw my frustration. 'What seems to be the trouble?' he asked. He leaned over the table. 'We used to live right here, near Rotterdam. That's where we saw the war begin.'

'Yes,' I said, 'I can find Rotterdam on this blank map. But look at all those other dots. Who's going to tell them apart?'

'It's not as difficult as you think,' my dad said, sitting down next to me. 'I know you can name some other cities in Holland, so let's start with those.'

Of course I knew Amsterdam, and The Hague, and, when I thought about it, Haarlem, and Delft, and Gouda.

'Well, you know those. Let's mark them off. Now the ones that are left over are just a few. Once you've got those, one by one, you've done it!'

He was right. It was easy! Actually, it was rather fun. I wondered if I might not only identify the cities and towns, but also most or all of the provinces on the blank map. Again, some were obvious: Limburg, where the first Dutch territory had been liberated, and Groningen, in the north, where my grandparents lived. My dad left me busy. I did not know it at the time, but we had had what was for me one of the most important conversations of my life.

During the next geography class I could not wait to demonstrate my newfound map skills, but did not get the chance; I was disappointed not to be called upon. The geography hour always seemed shorter than any other class. In any case, there was far too little geography during the week, I thought. Much more time was spent on all that dull history, on drawing and art, on language and literature, and on arithmetic. But geography, even from that awful textbook, was the highlight of my school day, and when the focus finally shifted from the Netherlands to the wider world, first to Europe and then to Asia and the Americas, my excitement grew by the week. In truth, I overdid it. My grades in other subjects were mediocre. Only in geography could I claim to be first in my class.

The more I learned about other cultures and natural environments, the more I wanted to see it all for myself. The walls of my room were covered with maps and photographs, and I started a crude filing system for information about countries and peoples. As it was, though, my activity space remained confined to the limits imposed by my bicycle. Had I taken to biology, that would have given me plenty to see, collect and describe; the Crown Domain alone was a paradise for nature observers. But starting geography by oneself is a daunting proposition, especially for a ten-year-old without much guidance outside the classroom.

I could, however, teach myself to read and use maps of the area I was able to reach by bike. Compared to the war years, this already was a wider world, encompassing not only Baarn but also Hilversum, where my father's radio studios were located, and Amersfoort, where I rode to see the war damage. The road to Hilversum lay through beautiful woods full of oak, pine, beech and birch trees. I liked that ride and loved the smells of the forest in the autumn. When I came to visit (and I am sure that it was not always at an opportune time) my father would allow me to sit in the rehearsal hall to listen to the orchestra. Afterward I would chart a different road back to Soestdijk, sometimes losing my way but learning to read my map more accurately

The road to Amersfoort was less pleasant, as the bike path lay right next to the busy highway the Amsterdam–Amersfoort road had become, and sometimes trucks and cars would crowd cyclists onto the shoulder. But Amersfoort was the nearest thing to a city I could reach, and I liked going there. In the autumn of 1945 there still was considerable war damage, but the main street was nearly back to normal, bustling with traffic, crowded with pedestrians, and lined with shops including some good bookshops. To get there, you passed the railway complex where the ammunition train had been hit by the Allied warplanes the previous spring. The burned-out hulks of freight cars were still there. Only when I made that first bike ride to Amersfoort, and saw its relative location on the map, was I aware just how close all this had been to our house and the village.

Soestdijk in the 1940s was not well connected to other places. There was a bus service between Baarn and Amersfoort that included a stop in our village, and when I did not ride my bike, this was the way I went to school. But the trains to Amsterdam went through Baarn, and trains to Rotterdam departed from Utrecht. Our village was comparatively isolated.

All this changed when an old friend of the village, Bello, resumed his service. Bello was the name affectionately bestowed on a single-track train that ran from the large station at Utrecht to Baarn, connecting several small villages, including Soestdijk, to these main lines. Bello consisted of a small steam locomotive and two or three antiquated cars with varnished walls and polished wooden seats. It lurched down the track like an elephant, and would arrive huffing and puffing at the tiny Soestdijk station every hour, ringing its bell to alert passengers. This museum piece was a godsend to the village, and in the mornings and late afternoons the cars would bulge with travellers connecting with other trains. I always enjoyed the hustle and bustle when I was in the vicinity during Bello's arrival. When the level-crossing barriers came down across the Amsterdam–Amersfoort road, there always was much honking from cars and bell-ringing from cyclists. The station was right beside the road, and Bello would depart, choof-choof-choof, far too slowly for the lengthening line of cars, bikes and pedestrians. Then the last carriage would pass, the barriers would rise, and for a few minutes the road was like a busy street in Rotterdam.

Just before the spring holidays in 1946, my mother asked me if I thought that I would be able to find my way from Bello's platform in Utrecht to the platform from which the trains to Rotterdam departed. I said that I was sure that I could, and a few days later I boarded Bello at midmorning, on my way to my aunt Sja's house in my favourite city.

For a ten-year-old, this was quite an adventure. Bello's platform in Utrecht was in a far corner of the city's huge railway station, and you had to walk up several flights of stairs to get to the main concourse. Then you had to look on the departure board for the location of the train to Rotterdam, and go through the ticket barrier. Armed with my map, I had followed Bello's stops along the way to Utrecht, but now the most exciting part of the journey began. The ride to Rotterdam aboard a fast, modern diesel train (no Bello, this) was a new experience. I was too young and impatient to see anything charming or picturesque in the pastures and canals, farmsteads and villages, rivers and windmills along the way. We went through small-town stations so fast that I could not read their names, and so I lost track of where we were on my map. But then the outskirts of the city appeared, and two railway lines multiplied into four, and then eight. The train slowed, and we passed apartment buildings and factories, saw trains going the other way and crossed bridges. Eventually we rode beneath a giant roof in the shape of a half-cylinder and stopped beside a long, crowded platform.

'When you get to the Central Station in Rotterdam,' my mother had said, 'cross the street and wait for tram number four. It goes along the Nieuwe Binnenweg and you'll recognize your aunt's house on the left.' That, too, was a challenge. The square in front of the station was a beehive of activity, and the trams all stopped in the middle of it. You had to negotiate cars, buses, bikes and trams coming from all directions to get to the tram stop. I took it slowly, and when I realized I had passed my aunt's house in the tram, I got off and walked back.

My aunt Sja was a remarkable woman. She never married, although she could count some prominent men among her suitors. She had a taste for travel and adventure, and one of her admirers, who owned a two-seater plane, made her one of Holland's first woman fliers. One especially rough landing broke the tip of the plane's propeller; she took it with her, had a clock installed in the centre and hung it over her fireplace, a reminder that she was not easily daunted.

Sja had exotic tastes. The interior walls of her house were grey, the woodwork black. Beautiful oriental carpets graced rooms and hallways. Her taste in art ranged from the classic to the avant-

111

garde, even the ultra-modern. Hundreds of books filled shelves in every room. Her furniture mixed antique and modern pieces, but the emphasis was on comfort. My favourite chair was by the living-room window on the first floor, overlooking the busy street.

I had not been in Sja's house since that frightening afternoon in 1940 when we got caught beneath machine-gunning planes, Now all was tranquil and peaceful, an oasis in the bustling city. But she was a busy woman, and left for work early in the morning. So I had the days to myself. I had prepared a schedule before I left Soestdijk, and now my first order of business was to get a good map of the city. This was a pleasant task, because wherever shops had been destroyed during the war, small, temporary kiosks had been set up where you could buy all sorts of small items. These tiny establishments specialized in such things as stamps, tobacco, small toys, pens and pencils, stationery and an endless variety of other goods. My pocket money would not go very far, but browsing was fun and watching the crowds was even better.

But my first order of business, on this and all subsequent trips to Rotterdam, was to go to the bank of the Maas River, to watch for some hours the incomparable spectacle of water traffic, reputedly the busiest in the world. From my favourite vantage point on a slope near where the Eurotower stands today, you could see hundreds of ships and boats, ranging from ocean liners and huge freighters to barges and tugs, navigating the crowded waters. Rows of barges, one attached to the next, lined the docks and extended into the river. Great cranes lifted enormous crates from ocean-going vessels onto smaller boats. Ferries loaded with passengers negotiated the busy traffic. Horns, whistles, and bells created a continuous cacophony. I never tired of the spectacle, and when it was time to leave, I was never ready to go.

My other priority was the zoo. The city zoo, where my father had introduced me to the wonders of wildlife had become a casualty of the war, but a new zoo named Blijdorp (what a felicitous name) was being created, and already part of it was open to the public. The enclosures were much more spacious than I remembered, and the elephant domain had an outside area lined with a moat and an inside pen where one could view the big pachyderms under cover. Of all the animals I liked the elephants best, as they always seemed to be communicating in some way with the people watching them, and with each other. They were so gentle for their size, sharing food, even resting their trunks on each other. I wondered whether their cooperativeness was the result of a shared sense of imprisonment, to make the best of circumstances that would never change.

This first visit to Rotterdam after the war was also my first chance to see close up the damage done by the bombardment of 1940, plus subsequent attacks and the German destruction visited upon the city, especially the port area, just before the Allies captured it. There still were mountains of rubble, skeletons of houses and other buildings, whole city blocks destroyed and cordoned off. The severely damaged St Laurens Cathedral still towered above the devastated city centre, its roofless frame now flanked by scaffolding.

I bought an old map of historic Rotterdam and began to record the devastated sectors. In the process I noted names I had heard my parents use so often years ago: the Willemsplein, the Great Market, the Kolkje, the Witte de Wit Street. On the map, the areas of total destruction dominated the whole inner city. Very little of what the map delimited as Historic Rotterdam in fact survived. Major buildings such as the City Hall and the Post Office had gaping holes in them where bombs had caved in the roof and walls, but other parts still stood. I coloured the devastated areas black and areas of partial destruction red, and in a few days had a pretty good image of the distribution of damage.

Some of the heaps of rubble were being removed by large groups of workers who seemed to crawl over them like ants and who carried bricks and planks and all else to waiting trucks and horse-drawn wagons. I fervently hoped that the old city would be reconstructed, and that the old street pattern on my map, with its cosy alleys and small squares, would be preserved But that, as I learned during subsequent visits, was not to be. While some major buildings were saved and reconstructed, including the venerable St Laurens Cathedral and its defiant tower, the heart of Rotterdam was bulldozed flat and modernized. A pedestrian mall with wide promenades flanked by outdoor cafes, called the Lijnbaan, rose in the city centre, linked to a new orchestra hall. On a prominent spot in the Lijnbaan stood a modern statue of a man with a large round hole in his torso, symbolizing what had happened to Rotterdam. I thought it perfectly reflected the new layout and architecture as well, a characterless expanse of glass and concrete that had all the cosiness of the inside of a refrigerator. Later, when faceless highrises rose around the perimeter of the Lijnbaan, the dehumanization of central Rotterdam, as far as I was concerned, was complete.

I got to know the city well enough, though, to discover neighbourhoods that had not been annihilated and where some of the atmosphere I treasured still survived. If Rotterdam had improved in any way since our departure in 1941, it was in its tram system. Every time I visited the city, the track network had expanded and new rolling stock had been added. You could buy an all-day pass and board the comfortable yellow streetcars to explore the city far and wide. You were safe in the busiest of traffic and could ride for miles in all directions, from the urban fringe where new apartment buildings were gobbling up farmlands to the Maas River waterfront where fishmongers sold salted herrings to waiting passengers.

The pace and energy of life in Rotterdam were stimulating and exciting, and whenever I got the chance, I made the trip. I always left the city with mixed feelings; to leave Rotterdam and, a few hours later, to climb off Bello in Soestdijk was to leave one world and readjust to another. Each visit, however yielded another map with new details of experiences and adventures, and these, posted in my room, formed my link to the world beyond.

F ew of us in the fifth form of the Nieuwe Baarnse School, I daresay, looked forward to advancing to the sixth form – the class taught by the redoubtable Mr van Dijk. Risking despatch to his office for one of his tongue-lashings was no one's idea of fun. But there we all were, in the autumn of 1946, wondering what the year would bring. In fact, Mr van Dijk seemed to have mellowed. We came to know him better as a fine teacher than as a menace. At the same time I learned something about some of my fellow students. A few boys in my class seemed determined to goad Mr van Dijk into one of his tirades, as though they actually wanted to go through the experience in his office. One of them succeed and returned to class with a roguish smile on his face.

I was determined to stay out of trouble. The highlights of the week were the three geography classes taught by Mr van Dijk and the music classes led by the first-form teacher, Miss Kort. The geography classes now dealt with Africa and the Pacific, no longer with the Netherlands – although the equally dull textbook was again written by old B. & F. But every week Mr van Dijk would come into class with a huge wall map of some new region of the world, and we learned about explorers and adventurers, some of them Dutch, as we studied countries and peoples. Among the books we had to acquire for the year was the new edition of the leading Dutch atlas, the Bos Atlas, a treasure I counted among my most prized possessions for years to come.

Every year, the sixth form presented an operetta for the parents and friends of the school. None of us, I think, thought much about that production, but in retrospect it was an amazing accomplishment. A new work was performed every year; sets were built, backdrops painted, songs rehearsed, dance routines prepared. Most of this was done after school hours. I sang in the school choir and had a leading part in the show, even having to dance a polka with a girl during the first act. Those previously free Wednesday afternoons were spent in assembly-hall practices. Toward the end of the school year, the show went on, and it was all worth it when the hall was filled with uncritical parents who loved every moment of it.

I especially enjoyed the music hour that came twice a week, on Tuesday and Thursday. We were given some basic music lessons, but mostly we sang long-forbidden songs about Dutch exploits, about the Dutch flag in distant lands, and about the virtues and beauties of the Netherlands itself.

One of these classes produced something of an irony. We practised several verses of the Dutch national anthem, and much emphasis was placed on enunciation. Getting the words right led me to pay attention to what the anthem actually said. The language refers to the 'honouring' of a Spanish king, a legacy from the time when Spain was the dominant power in Holland. But in my history classes I was learning how ruthless Spanish rule had been, and about the cruelties inflicted on the Dutch by Spain's armies. Hollanders at the time must have regarded the Spaniards the same way we looked upon the Germans. Why were we singing these ridiculous words about honouring a Spanish king?

I asked the music teacher about this. 'It's ancient history,' she said. 'The Dutch are a very adaptable people. It's one of our strong points. We don't mind letting bygones be bygones, and that's how you get along in the world.'

That was not good enough for me. Imagine singing the praises of Hitler a few hundred years hence! I talked it over with Bernhard, who by now was in the fifth form at another school. 'Well,' he said, 'the Spaniards did do some good, the Nazis didn't. They brought the Roman Catholic religion here. We're Catholic, and so are most of the people in the village. So for that reason alone, what we sing in the anthem isn't all bad.'

That gave me pause. Were we Hollanders first, or Catholics first? My parents were not churchgoers, although my mother had been brought up in a nominally Catholic family. My father had never conveyed his agnostic views to me, and in fact he had brought home, just after the war, a children's bible with the suggestion that I read some of it every night. I had been doing that, but had difficulty understanding why God's capacity to perform miracles was not used to stop war, save lives and feed the hungry. After the war I also overheard tense discussions about Catholic collaboration with the Nazis and even the possibility that Roman Catholic monasteries in Italy were used to help Nazi war criminals escape to countries in South America. On a few occasions I had gone to the Catholic church in the village centre with the Batenburg children, and once to the Protestant church up the street, and found myself uncomfortable with ceremony and ritual. I was particularly surprised by the unchristian vehemence with which Catholics and Protestants seemed to malign each other. Organized religion, I decided quite early, was not for me.

But few of my sixth-form days were clouded by such serious matters. I played goalkeeper for the school soccer team, which reconvened during the holidays to practise wherever we could find a field, practised my violin just enough to satisfy my father, and

116

managed to persuade my mother to let me give up my piano lessons. That was a terrible mistake I came to regret enormously in later years, but I had no great talent for music and preferred the violin. My father got me a place in the regional symphony orchestra and later that year I sat among the second violins for my first public performance.

What a difference freedom made during the winter months! Now we were out skating and sledging, coal fires burned in the stoves of every room in the house, and snowfalls were things of beauty, not harbingers of cold and misery. Bobby was getting fat in her middle age, and her puppy Loebas, too, was getting big. They raced through the Crown Domain, and in the thick snow, all you could sometimes see were two tails rising like periscopes from the white surface.

Spring transformed the Crown Domain into a sea of colours, and I loved my bike rides to and from school. These were my final weeks at the Nieuwe Baarnse School, and another transition loomed. But first there were examinations and farewells. Mr van Dijk and his staff made the last school day a truly memorable experience. For him this was a special class because of what had happened during the war. His address to the packed assembly hall described the passage of this class from the day the Nazi officers had come to his office to announce their plans to oust him, his staff and his pupils, to this joyous day when the future was so bright. Then, suddenly, he could speak no further, got out his handkerchief, and walked to the side of the podium. Mr Vermeer concluded the ceremony. I looked down the row of my classmates. Most looked open-mouthed at the stage. No one had realized that the formidable headmaster could be overcome by his emotions this way.

Most of the students in the Nieuwe Baarnse School aspired to go to a private high school called the Beams Lyceum, reputed to be one of the three best high schools in the country. And while most of them managed to enter the Lyceum, there was no guarantee, even for students with high grades. The Lyceum required a rigorous, three-hour examination to be taken by all

117

applicants, some of whom came from distant towns to attempt it. On a midsummer Saturday I biked to the examination site, a cavernous hall in Baarn filled with seemingly endless rows of desks.

When I arrived and saw the sea of faces, almost as far as the eye could reach, my heart sank. But once I got seated and saw the examination paper, my spirits rose. This looked easy! I plunged in, and about 70 minutes later was finished with what was scheduled to be a three-hour examination. I looked around, and could see everyone else still bent over the paper. I checked some of the arithmetic again, and of course the geography. Then my impatience got the better of me; I got up and handed in my work. The proctor looked at his watch, shook his head, noted the time on my paper and pointed to the exit door.

When I got home, my mother at first thought that the examination had been cancelled. What was I doing home so soon? I told her that I had finished early and what was the point of sitting there, looking at my test? She shook her head. 'Why are you always in such a hurry? This may cost you your chance to get into the Lyceum!'

She was right, and she was not the last to point out to me that slowing down has its merits. But I never could, then or later in life. I always worked, ran, biked, played and practised as fast as I could, often faster than was good for me. I know that it drove my dad, still trying to improve my violin-playing, to distraction. I know it irritated teachers, friends, and colleagues throughout my life. I tried, but I never was able to do much about it. I always had what seemed to be boundless energy, sometimes too much of it. Often I benefited from it, but at other times it contributed to poor or hasty judgment.

Fortunately my mother's fears were unjustified. About three weeks after the examination I received notification of my admission to the first-year class of the Baarns Lyceum. And there my encounter with geography would take a fateful turn.

10

FATE

Preparing for the Baarns Lyceum was nothing like what it was for the Nieuwe Baarnse School. For one, you had to get your own supplies, from notebooks to textbooks. For the art class alone, it was brushes, special paper, paints, coloured pencils, ruler, and more. For the geography class you were advised to buy a globe and an atlas 'for personal reference at home', along with two textbooks. One of the texts dealt with the Netherlands, the other with world geography.

My experience in Mr van Dijk's geography classes had been mixed. I liked the parts about Africa and the Pacific, but the study of the Netherlands had been pretty routine and dull. I loved looking at maps and trying to draw my own, but some of the homework exercises seemed to be mostly a listing of ports and products. So I was eager to experience the geography class at the Baarns Lyceum, because it would be a new beginning and probably a more challenging course. (I dreaded the art class, remembering my time in the 'atelier' of the Nieuwe Baarnse School. At least we did not have to buy any clay...)

When I pedalled to my new school on a Monday morning early in the autumn, the leaves in the Crown Domain were already turning, and the forest, moist with morning fog, smelled earthy. The newly whitewashed royal palace, again the home of the royal family, glimmered in the light of dawn. The sound of the gravel on the bike path crunching under my tyres was all that broke the silence. I was embarking on a whole new adventure and could not wait to get it started.

From the first moment I could tell that this would be a different life. At our first assembly in the school's great hall, we were given class schedules and rules of behaviour. Unlike the Nieuwe Baarnse School, where teachers came to one's classroom, we were to walk from room to room. Every teacher had his or her own classroom, and we were described as 'visitors' for the hour of instruction. As luck would have it, my first class, during the second hour of this initial day, was a geography class.

I quickly found the geography classroom and got a seat in the first row. Looking around, I saw that this was no ordinary classroom; it was more like a private office with about two dozen desks in it. Maps, charts and diagrams covered every wall. The teacher's desk, facing the classroom, was a real office desk loaded with books and papers. Bookshelves lined the front wall of the classroom. Globes large and small stood on the floor and on stacks of manuscript.

The geography teacher was Mr E. de Wilde (not until much later did I learn that the E stood for Eric). In the unfortunately brief time I would have at the Baarns Lyceum, he set my life on a course from which I never deviated.

Mr de Wilde was, in fact, no spellbinding lecturer. But he was a consummate teacher. He was, he told us, teaching because he enjoyed it, and because geography was the greatest field you could study. In fact, he could have retired on his 'little pension' from a period of work in the Dutch East Indies. But he would rather teach. And he had a warning. 'Geography is not easy,' he said. 'Don't fall behind in your reading.'

Mr de Wilde had taught at schools in Batavia (now Jakarta) and Bandung, and he had studied and travelled all over South-East Asia. Occasionally he would leave the topic of the day and digress into an anecdote about his time in the tropics. He had been through two tropical cyclones, had been covered by ash from a volcanic eruption, had felt the earth shake. He was in Java when the Japanese took control of the Dutch East Indies, and was interned. Then, after the war, the Indonesians rebelled and the Dutch tried to regain their former colony by force of arms. He was caught in that crossfire too, and reluctantly left for Holland. That was why we were now meeting in this classroom. Around us were many of the

120

memorabilia Mr de Wilde had brought back with him, a tale attached to almost every one.

Mr de Wilde was no mere storyteller, however. He required more homework than any of our other teachers, and his tests were tough. But no one complained. Often, when he had covered a country in class, we were so excited by what he had told us that we would use the first available free hour to head for the library to learn more about it, or to a nearby travel agency to get brochures on it. I am still not sure how he did it, but no teacher ever inspired me more. As I learned much later, I was not the only one in that class who became addicted to geography to the point of making it a career.

For some years I had been building a filing system on countries of the world; now I added geographic topics such as urbanization, migration, transport and others. That filing system was very useful, because Mr de Wilde required frequent reports on countries, provinces, regions or current developments in the world that had geographic dimensions. Such reports could not be submitted without maps, charts and, if available, photographs. I learned to scour magazines for maps and pictures of geographic relevance. Mr de Wilde was invariably interested in what I and others had found, but he also was critical. What you presented had to be geographic. 'Always ask yourself,' he urged, 'why you are presenting that map or that photograph. How does it inform rather than merely illustrate?'

The geography hour always was too short, especially when it was followed by the class of other teachers who were far less inspiring. Our English teacher was an old, distinguished gentleman whose room had one shelf of books in it and whose desk was bare save for one pen and one pencil; he told us that he would soon speak to us only in English, and shortly we would be compelled to do the same. Our French teacher was a caricature Frenchman, a broken-down opera singer who was still performing – in class, so it seemed. Our German teacher was a huge and domineering woman who had the unenviable task of teaching the language of people we all detested. I took an instant dislike to the art teacher, a

121

mean little man who made us do watercolours and ridiculed those who could not get them right. But undoubtedly the most memorable figure was the mathematics teacher, Mr Munzenbrock, whose classroom was always in chaos and from whom we learned very little.

The Baarns Lyceum in those days was located right next to the railway line very near the Baarn station, and directly across from the local station of Bello. The railway lines formed the main artery from Amsterdam eastwards and trains passed almost continuously. In 1947, both streamlined diesel trains and trains pulled by huge old puffing steam locomotives shared the tracks.

Mr Munzenbrock's first-floor classroom overlooked those tracks, because he loved trains, not mathematics. We would settle down at our desks, he would begin a discourse on some mathematical problem (his mumbling seemed to be made worse by his unkempt moustache, which hung over his mouth so you could neither hear nor see what he was saying), and then a train would rumble past. 'Look at that' he would shout. 'That's a nineteen-thirty-three Frügenstücker locomotive, the most advanced of its time! It can pull sixty loaded freight cars!' And then he would launch into an ode to this or some other behemoth of the rails. We, of course, loved it. While embarked on one of his monologues, Mr Munzenbrock would issue no homework requirements. Often he would still be at it when the bell rang, and we would rush off before he could give us an assignment.

As my first half-year at the Baarns Lyceum progressed, I was not, to put it mildly, at the top of my class. In November came the first parent-teacher evening, and I well remember the look on my mother's face when she came in the kitchen door. It had been a difficult experience for them, that much was obvious. They made no bones about it: I had excelled in one subject and had dissatisfied the teachers in all the others, especially in art. 'He has no talent, zero, zip,' the art teacher had told my parents, no strangers to the arts. Fortunately my father liked the art teacher about as much as I did, but my mother said that I had obviously not tried my best. 'Languages are obviously not his strong point,' opined the French teacher (the English teacher was slightly less generous). 'Better get him some remedial education,' mumbled Mr Munzenbrock.

122

In truth, I had been unaware that I was doing as badly as all that. But when my first report card arrived in the mail two weeks later, there could be no doubt. I had what amounted to an A in geography and nothing above a D in anything else.

Now things changed. From the first week of January 1948, I went for two hours of private lessons in mathematics at the home of a retired teacher, who helped me keep up with what Mr Munzenbrock was (and was not) teaching. My father, who spoke French fluently, required a daily progress report on my French classes and went over my homework with me. My mother checked every assignment with which I came home. I was pretty much confined to the house until my grades improved. And geography would just have to take a back seat for a while.

But instead, Mr de Wilde's geography class became an oasis, the highlight of the day. I wished that I could spend the entire school day, not just one period, in that classroom filled with fascinating things. I wondered what Mr de Wilde's more advanced geography classes were like, and I asked to see the textbooks for those courses. He willingly obliged, and I saw that there would be classes devoted entirely to climate and weather, to the formation of the natural landscape, and to specific parts of the world such as Africa and Asia. It was an exciting prospect.

Still, I knew that I would have to improve my grades in other classes, or there would be no advanced geography for me. Slowly but surely I got better marks in English, French and mathematics, and my science and history grades also went up. But it was difficult to devote as much time as I should to these subjects when there was always geography to do. As for the art class, I got a huge break. My mother, on the train from Amsterdam, sat in the same compartment as Mr Ingels, the art teacher. They had a conversation and my mother apparently made an impression. Suddenly the jokes about my dismal art work stopped, and my grades went up a bit. There was obviously a lesson in this, but not one you learned in class.

At dinner one evening I told my parents that I wanted to be a geographer, if possible a teacher like Mr de Wilde. 'It's a little early for you to be talking about career decisions,' said my father. 'And remember, everything else you're studying is relevant to your geography, so don't put all your eggs in one basket.' He was right, but I was hooked. Fortunately the French teacher had been wrong: I did have some talent for foreign languages, and eventually I learned to speak four of them fluently. But I had a weakness in mathematics no remedial work seemed to be able to overcome. That would be a lifelong handicap.

I remember wondering, during these early high-school days, whether my weaknesses in mathematics and music ware somehow related. My violin-playing was passable, but no more than that, and only with daily practising and far more attention from my father than any ordinary student of it could expect. Were the really smart people in this world those who were good at mathematics or music, or both? I asked my father about this. Einstein was a great mathematician, he said, but as an amateur violinist he was, well, rather poor. Still, if you took music (I mean serious music, for which you need theory, practice, and competence under performance conditions) and mathematics, they had a good deal in common. Music theory deals in mathematical fractions and rhythmic variations you also encounter in mathematics. I wished I was better at both, or even either.

One aspect of geography I liked, and it was diametrically opposed to the specifics of mathematics and music, was the way it formulated an overall image of the world, or a region, or a process from many kinds of sometimes disparate information. In Mr de Wilde's class I could not count the number of times I said to myself 'Ah, so *that's* how this works!' I learned that warmth from the tropics, carried northward by ocean currents, gave us our mild climate; that America's Great Lakes were diked by ice sheets; that the (still) Dutch East Indies had so many islands because they were formed by volcanoes sticking up above the sea, and were so populous because volcanic soil was fertile. Mr de Wilde knew the world and ranged across it like a global pundit: his history was better than we had in history class, his geology related to resources and people (unlike our science class), his examples ranged from Antarctica to Lapland. 'Always remember to look for connections,' he would say. 'This is a shrinking world. What you and your parents eat, drink or purchase for your homes affects producers and workers around the globe.' It was not, I think, what high

124

school students were hearing in their geography classes in most of the world. He was ahead of his time.

Mr de Wilde also challenged us to generalize in other ways. Could we come up with an average layout for a village in the Province of Utrecht? What features would you find in the average European city? I do not think he ever used the term, but he taught us the idea of what today we call modelling, the creation of models representing many things from villages to transport systems. Models are indispensable today in urban and regional planning and in a host of other geographic arenas. And he wanted us to use our geographic knowledge to predict. Would Rotterdam become a bigger city than Amsterdam, and why or why not? Would New York always remain the world's largest city? Would Japan become a major force in East Asia? (He thought it would, despite the devastation of the war including two atomic bombs. The Japanese, he told us, had demonstrated that it is people and their abilities, not domestic resources, that make for economic and political power.)

Mr de Wilde involved us in such discussions as though we were adults, and made us think about the postwar world as though we could actually affect its fate. There were times when I left his class unable to concentrate on the next one because so many things were going through my mind. When the final grades for the year were posted, my only A was in geography. But at least I had done well enough to be promoted to the second year.

In the meantime, exciting changes were going on at home. My parents' musical careers were soaring, and new furniture and paintings appeared in our living, dining and music rooms. The patio at the back of the house was enlarged, and new garage doors allowed the 1934 Wolseley to be parked inside.

The Wolseley was what you would expect: trouble. It had been owned by someone in a nearby town who had hidden it from the Germans in a farmer's barn, where it had stood on blocks, covered under hay. What remained of its paint, a dark green with a black top, showed streaks of wear and only patches of sheen. The windscreen consisted of two layers between which there was some sort of glue that had turned brown, blotching it and making it hard to see through. The engine was a mess of oily wires in bunches, many loose ends going nowhere. The tyres were, to be generous, balding. But the old bomb was my father's pride and joy. When it ran, which by (again generous) estimate was half the time, it signified success and freedom.

The Wolseley certainly expanded our activity space, and my parents used every available day to visit (by Dutch standards) far-away places. We visited my grandparents in Groningen, and it was the only car parked on the street. We took a camping trip to Limburg, where I had difficulty understanding the Dutch they spoke (but in the Province of Friesland I could not understand it at all). We visited Sja in Rotterdam. Wherever we went, I followed our route on maps, and drew my own as part of my record of the trip. Mr de Wilde had told us always to remember the scale at which we were looking at things, and I enjoyed reporting to him on these excursions by showing him my maps.

But there were other changes of which I knew nothing. My father had been hearing from colleagues in various parts of the world – in Canada, Venezuela, South Africa, Australia – who had left Holland after the war and were doing well in their new environment. He and my mother had been discussing the prospect that they would also emigrate. In South Africa, where there was quite a large group of Dutch musicians in orchestras in Johannesburg, Durban and Cape Town, they spoke a language not unlike Dutch, lived in comfort in large houses, enjoyed a sunny climate, and had many professional and personal opportunities. Several of these colleagues had written my father about coming to South Africa to take a chair as first violinist in the Johannesburg City Orchestra, then the country's leading symphony in its largest city.

So it was that one early autumn day in 1948, just before the first school day of my second year at the Baarns Lyceum, my mother met me at the Soestdijk railway station as I returned from a trip to Rotterdam. That was unusual, and I was pleasantly surprised. 'Let's walk the scenic road past the Eng,' she said. 'I have something important to tell you.'

We walked along a pavement lined with large, leafy oak trees that had survived the German retreat because the road past the Eng had not been a strategic route. I began to tell her about my trip from Utrecht on Bello. Some boys had thrown stones at the train and broken a window in the car in which I was riding.

My mother did not seem to be listening. 'I have big news for you,' she said as we walked along. 'Your father has accepted a position in an orchestra in South Africa. We will be leaving in a few months. We will be living in a city called Johannesburg.'

I felt as if a bolt of lightning had struck me on a clear day. So many thoughts flooded into my head that I could barely speak. 'That ... that will mean ... a complete turnaround in my life, won't it?' I stammered. What, I wondered, about the dogs, my friends, Sja, Mr de Wilde?

'More than you realize now. Mine, too,' my mother said.

'What about Bobby and Loebas?'

'They'll have to stay here. A couple named Mr and Mrs Visser are interested in our house. They say that they may take Bobby and Loebas so they can stay in their own home. That's best for them. They'll be in familiar surroundings and they won't miss us as much as they otherwise would.'

Tears welled up in my eyes. Bobby and Loebas had become such a large part of my life that being without them was just inconceivable. And what if they did not like these people?

'Can we maybe come and get them when we have a house down there?'

'No,' my mother said. 'It would be impractical. There are very strict quarantine laws and they would be locked up in separate cages for six months. Bobby is no youngster any more. She probably wouldn't survive it.'

We walked along in silence, and I saw that my mother, too, wiped away a tear. The full meaning of what she had told me still was incomprehensible. I would be leaving that wonderful house, my room full of things from rock samples to stamps. I wondered whether I would be able to take my globe and maps and books. And I might never see Bernard and Paul again!

And what about Mr de Wilde and my geography classes? I already had the books for the second year, and now I would not even do the course!

When we got home I looked up South Africa in the Bos Atlas. Our encyclopedia contained a photograph of Johannesburg. 'Far from the sea,' I commented. 'No rivers nearby.'

'Yes, but that's not important,' my mother said. 'There's quite a large Dutch community there, and we'll feel at home. Your father's friends say they like it in Johannesburg. And many of the people speak a language that's not too different from ours.

'Your father has another reason to want to move to South Africa,' she continued. 'But I will let him tell you about that himself.'

My father came home late that afternoon and he knew that I had been told the news. 'South Africa,' he said, 'has the most magnificent nature preserve in the world, the Kruger National Park. We're going to take our car and as soon as we can we'll go there. Think about it. Elephants and lions not in cages, but in the wild.'

I would believe it when I saw it. Meanwhile, I had to report to the Rector of the Baarns Lyceum that I would be missing some classes as our preparations for departure progressed.

'South Africa?' said Mr Driessen. 'You are going to the Union? That country has always been a dream of mine. Write me some time when you are in Johannesburg.'

At least the Rector had a positive reaction to my news. Mr de Wilde had his doubts. 'That's a country in transition,' he said. 'They're embarking on some worrisome social policies. You never know what's going to happen there. It isn't really a colony, but in some ways it is like one, and the future of such countries is uncertain. Has your father gone down there to look the situation over? Anyway, good luck and I'll miss you. You were a good student in my class.'

Of course my father had not visited South Africa, but I trusted his judgment totally. Still, it was obvious that none of my friends was impressed. What was so great about South Africa? Do they play football there? Can you ride a bike? Can you get food like we eat here? I was surprised that so many of my friends were totally uninterested in my adventure. Long before I could have expected it, here I was on the eve of the kind of world voyage I had dreamed of when reading van Loon in those last months of the war.

It was difficult to concentrate on school during the final months of my life in the Netherlands, but I tried never to miss any of Mr de Wilde's geography classes. He let me read what materials he had on South Africa, and predicted – accurately, as it turned out – that my South African school might not offer geography as a subject.

128

'Don't lose your enthusiasm,' he said. 'Even if you cannot take geography in high school, you *will* be able to pursue it at college. And let me tell you. What I do is the best job there is.'

I thought about those words when the KLM DC–4 took off from Schiphol Airport towards what was then Johannesburg's air terminal, Palmietfontein. I was determined to heed them, and did.

And he was right. I cannot imagine a better life than that of a geographer.